The Celtic Breeze

World Folklore Advisory Board

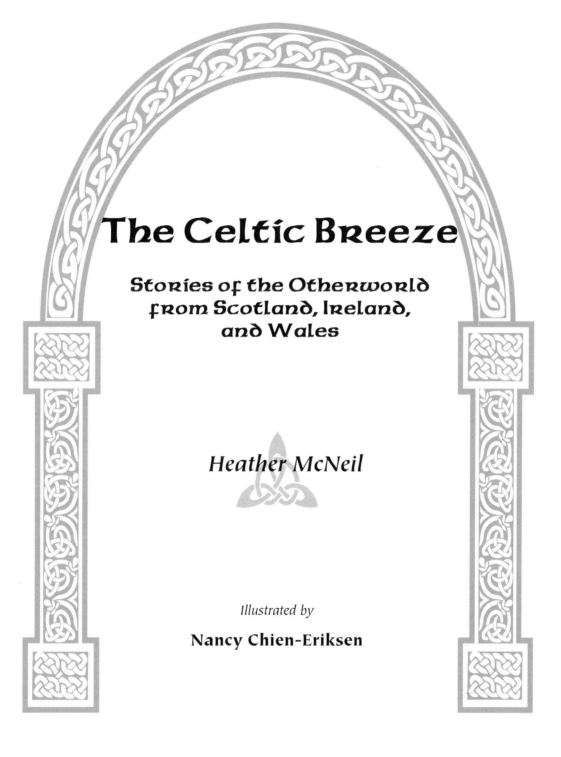

The Celtic Breeze

Stories of the Otherworld from Scotland, Ireland, and Wales

Heather McNeil

Illustrated by

Nancy Chien-Eriksen

2001
LIBRARIES UNLIMITED
A Division of Greenwood Publishing Group, Inc.
Englewood, Colorado

Libraries Unlimited
A Division of Greenwood Publishing Group, Inc.
P.O. Box 6633
Englewood, CO 80155-6633
1-800-237-6124
www.lu.com

Library of Congress Cataloging-in-Publication Data

McNeil, Heather.
    The Celtic breeze: stories of the otherworld from Scotland, Ireland, and Wales /
Heather McNeil.
        p. cm. -- (World folklore series)
    Includes bibliographical references and index.
    ISBN 1-56308-778-2
    1. Celts--Folklore. 2. Fairy tales--Scotland. 3. Fairy tales--Ireland. 4. Fairy
tales--Wales. I. Title. II. Series.

GR137 .M33 2001
398.2'089'916--dc21   2001029622

The Celtic Breeze is dedicated to my nephews, Ryan and Dana, because they are the next generation of McNeils to pass on the stories.

It is also dedicated to the memory of my father, a Celtic warrior who knew the true meaning of chivalry.

World Folklore Series

Folk Stories of the Hmong: Peoples of Laos, Thailand, and Vietnam. By Norma J. Livo and Dia Cha.

Images of a People: Tlingit Myths and Legends. By Mary Helen Pelton and Jacqueline DiGennaro.

Hyena and the Moon: Stories to Tell from Kenya. By Heather McNeil.

The Corn Woman: Stories and Legends of the Hispanic Southwest. Retold by Angel Vigil.

Thai Tales: Folktales of Thailand. Retold by Supaporn Vathanaprida. Edited by Margaret Read MacDonald.

In Days Gone By: Folklore and Traditions of the Pennsylvania Dutch. By Audrey Burie Kirchner and Margaret R. Tassia.

From the Mango Tree and Other Folktales from Nepal. By Kavita Ram Shrestha and Sarah Lamstein.

Why Ostriches Don't Fly and Other Tales from the African Bush. By I. Murphy Lewis.

The Magic Egg and Other Tales from Ukraine. Retold by Barbara J. Suwyn. Edited by Natalie O. Kononenko.

When Night Falls, Kric! Krac! Haitian Folktales. By Liliane Nérette Louis. Edited by Fred J. Hay.

Jasmine and Coconuts: South Indian Tales. By Cathy Spagnoli and Paramasivam Samanna.

The Enchanted Wood and Other Folktales from Finland. By Norma J. Livo and George O. Livo.

A Tiger by the Tail and Other Stories from the Heart of Korea. Retold by Lindy Soon Curry. Edited by Chan-eung Park.

The Eagle on the Cactus: Traditional Stories from Mexico. Retold by Angel Vigil.

Tales from the Heart of the Balkans. Retold by Bonnie C. Marshall. Edited by Vasa D. Mihailovich.

The Celtic Breeze: Stories of the Otherworld from Scotland, Ireland, and Wales. By Heather McNeil.

Selections Available on Audiocassette

Hyena and the Moon: Stories to Tell from Kenya.

The Corn Woman: Stories and Legends of the Hispanic Southwest.

Thai Tales: Folktales of Thailand.

Folk Stories of the Hmong: Peoples of Laos, Thailand, and Vietnam.

✖ Contents

Part I
The Faery Folk of the Earth

Part II
The Faery Folk of the Water

Color Photographs

Part III
The Faery Folk and Ghosts

Part IV
The Faery Folk and Music

# Preface

Every inch . . . was alive with legends and otherworld beings. Mysterious tales made the caves and the kirkyard a terror by night; the sealwoman crooned on the reefs; the mermaid bathed in the creeks; the fairies sang and piped in the knolls; the water-sprite washed in a certain burn the shrouds of the dying; the kelpie hatched plots in the tarns against beautiful maidens. . . . Within doors, however, at the ceilidh, the folk told the tales and sang the ballads of the Fayne, or of the less ancient heroes . . . with, for Sundays and holy days, beautiful legends of Iona and Oronsay. But ever, whether on holy or on other eve, as midnight drew nearer, the tales and the songs, and the distant roar of the Western Sea grew weirder, until at last song and tale ceased, and the fire smouldered, and the cruisie-light flickered, and the folk whispered, while over the ceilidh crept the shadow of night and the mysteries hiding therein. (Macleod, p. xxxviii)

My retellings of sixteen ancient stories are of that Celtic faery world and of those mortals who have been touched by its shadow and mystery. They are the stories of my ancestors. Celts, Vikings, landlords, chiefs, fishermen, weavers, bards, wives waiting for their husbands to return from sea, children looking for the faery folk in the heather, grandparents gathering their family around a peat fire to listen to the tales—these are the stories they told.

My ancestors come from the Isle of Barra, one of the Outer Hebrides Islands of Scotland. They descend from the Irish High King, Niall of the Nine Hostages, who, legend says, survived being abandoned by his stepmother as an infant and was raised by a wandering bard. He and his four brothers were sent into a burning forge and, because Niall came out with the anvil, the smith foretold he would be king. As a child, I was also told of another ancestor, O'Neal of Tyrone, who was contending against his brother for the kingship of an Ulster island. Whoever touched land first would rule. When he got close enough, O'Neal cut off his hand and threw it onto the shore, thus creating the legend of the "Red Hand of Ulster," and the symbol that is on our family's crest.

The MacNeils have been on the Isle of Barra since the twelfth century, and I grew up with the stories of their battles and their fame. A former Chief's Herald was known to announce from the top of the Great Tower of Kisimul Castle:

Hear O ye People and listen all ye nations,
The great Macneil of Barra having finished his meal,
The Princes of the world may now dine.

In October 1994, I traveled to Barra to listen to and record the stories. I expected to hear glorious tales of the chiefs of the clan and magical stories of faeries that still flitted about in the early morning mist. I heard neither. What I did hear were jokes, haunted house stories, tales remembered by a teacher who used to read to her students, and theories about where the idea of faeries came from. I heard Calum McNeil, Castlebay's expert on the history of the clan, say, "We were not nice people," when he spoke of the greedy landlords who decided owning sheep was more profitable than allowing people to continue living in their "black houses," so named because of the effects of coal smoke. Those were the days of the Highland Clearances, when thousands of farmers and fishermen were forced to leave Scotland and find new homes in Canada, Ireland, or the United States. Many did not survive the journey.

I heard about the weather, and the long, cold, wet winters. I heard about how John Allen MacNeil's wife had recently died, and how Morag MacAulay came to be known as "The Fair Maid of Barra." Everyone was talking about the Mod, a national competition of Gaelic singing, and how the children of Barra were doing in the contest. In other words, I heard the usual stories told around the world by members of a community. Every elder I spoke with pointed to the television and said, "That's why the stories are gone. The children don't listen anymore."

But every once in a while there would be a "wee tale" given to me, an idea or a memory of a story heard long ago. Those stories grew like seeds in my soul. With the nourishment of research and the light of imagination, I found my own tellings of those tales, which I have written in this book. I was also led to the discovery of other stories, hidden in obscure books no longer read because of their format or no longer in print because of their age or limited appeal. For me, they were treasure far more valuable than the leprechaun's gold.

It is important to recognize that the focus of the Scottish stories in this collection is on the Highlands, a distinction that was more significant in the past than it is in the present. An understanding of that period of Scottish history is useful for interpreting the emotional tone or attitude of the stories.

As early as 1380, in the writings of John of Fordun, a Lowland Aberdeenshire chronicler, the Lowlanders were described as "trusty, patient and urbane, decent in their attire, affable and peaceful." He depicted the Highlanders and Islanders as "rude and independent, given to rapine, easy-living . . . comely in person but unsightly in dress, hostile to the English people and language, and, owing to diversity of speech, even to their own nation, and exceedingly cruel."

The Lowlanders spoke Scots, a version of Middle English, and the Highlanders spoke Gaelic. This diversity was considered to be the root of their differences, and it coincided with a north and south division created by the hills. For another 400 years that image of barbaric versus civilized continued, until the nineteenth century, when many Scots began to adopt traditional Highland symbols, such as the kilt and tartan, bagpipe, and sprig of heather. Other occurrences, such as Sir Walter Scott's romantic writings about the Highlanders and the popularity of the Glasgow Police Band, which was made up predominantly of Highland recruits, contributed to the creation of the stereotypical Scot: stubborn, defiant, dressed in a kilt, and either playing the bagpipes or drinking ale.

In spite of the rising popularity of that image, Highland society was actually diminishing. The failure of the Jacobite risings in 1715 and 1745 was significant, but equally important was a hostile government determined to minimize the importance of the Gaelic culture. Highland landowners began to clear out the peasant farms, which brought them little revenue, and during the first half of the nineteenth century, the Lowlander and his sheep, which brought more of a profit, took over the land. The Gaelic language declined, retaining popularity only in the Outer Hebrides and a few other communities.

The division and characteristics of Highlander and Lowlander became less obvious. Today, being a Lowlander refers more to religious affiliation, coming from Edinburgh rather than Glasgow, or even backing a particular football team. Being a Highlander is even less definitive—except in the Inner and Outer Hebrides. The power of the Gaelic language in the Western Isles, such as Barra, is much less diminished. The islands have a history of "crofting communities," comprised of small-scale farms, sometimes combined with fishing or weaving. They have survived due to their right to hand on their holdings to their heirs, thanks to the Crofters Holding Act of 1886. *Insight Guides: Scotland* describes today's Highlanders as follows:

> [T]he Highland way of life . . . can best be understood in Scotland by a journey to the Outer Hebrides. . . . [T]he Gaelic tradition in many respects defies the dominant world outside. . . . The Highlander is often unmodern in priorities, is materialistic yet with little sense of individual ambition, attaches little importance to clock-watching. . . .

Gaelic society is supportive of its members, has an abiding sense of kinship and an unembarrassed love of a song and a story, as it has an unembarrassed love of drink. (Smout, p. 68)

This is the tradition and the history of the Scottish stories included in *The Celtic Breeze*.

I have also included two stories from Celtic Ireland. The legend of "Niall of the Nine Hostages," ancestor of the MacNeils, is intriguing because of its similarity to the legend of King Arthur, another hero who appears in Welsh history several hundred years later. "Oisean of the Finne" is the other story with ancient Irish roots, but it is also frequently attributed to the Highlands of Scotland.

My mother's ancestors were from Cornwall and Wales. The Welsh were miners and farmers, the people of the earth, and they, too, passed down tales of the faery folk, dragons, and a passion for the unseen and the impossible. I have included two Welsh tales, "Lady of the Lake" and "The Buried Moon." Wales is also the land of King Arthur and his Knights of the Round Table. I have stood on the cliffs of Tintagel, the castle where Arthur was supposedly born, and looked down through the mist and fog to see the cave where Merlin is said to have hidden the boy on that stormy night. I have walked the quiet paths of Glastonbury, where Arthur and his Guinevere are said to be buried; I have read the many books about those dark and golden years, both fact and fiction; and I have chosen to believe the magic of the legend. I have come to believe in the Otherworld, and I hope that someday I will turn around quickly enough to see one of its inhabitants, preferably one with mischief, not malice, on its mind. When I sang to the seals of Barra I seriously considered returning to the rocky shores by moonlight, for in my heart I knew the selkies would be dancing there. I am always on the lookout for rings of toadstools and fields of bluebells, which are known to be places of faery spells and enchantments. It is through believing in the power of magic, both good and evil, that we are able to accept the possibility of all miracles in our stories.

While I was collecting stories I stayed at the home of Donald Angus and Mary Sarah MacNeil in Castlebay. They run a bed and breakfast called *Ceol Mara* (kyohl MAH-rah), which is Gaelic for "sea music." Mary Sarah took great care of me, spoiling me with delicious breakfasts of broiled tomatoes, oat cakes, and vegetable patties, and with pancakes and jam in the parlor each afternoon for tea. She washed my clothes, took me to a meeting of the clan, and put me in touch with those who might give me stories. She also worried about me, for I was often gone adventuring longer than she expected. On the first day of my visit, my "few hours" of walking along the coast became an entire afternoon and evening of raking, cleaning, cooking, and eating cockles with two fellows who invited me to join them on Cocklestrand Beach. Mary Sarah called almost everyone on the island to find out what had happened to me, and for the rest of my days in Castlebay I was greeted with, "Oh, you're the one that Mary Sarah was afraid had fallen into the sea."

Mary Sarah also became a friend, and we shared many conversations about our very different lives. She has always lived on Barra and married a man who is about twenty years her senior. He is often away at sea, so she runs *Ceol Mara*. She has no children but enjoys the company of her two nieces, Rosemarie and Kerryann, and their friend, Jennifer. They are delightful girls; here's what I wrote about them in my journal:

> *Rosemarie, age 8, is a beauty, with dark curly hair that wisps about her face, blue eyes surrounded by thick lashes. She's quiet, and not comfortable with being the center of attention. Kerryann is 9, chubby, with the same beautiful blue eyes as her sister, and very clever with remembering my stories and voices. Jennifer is 6, an imp, full of giggles and tricks. She is blonde, with a round face and blue eyes, and she still has a touch of the preschooler who wants favorite stories and songs repeated, and who interrupts willy-nilly with sudden thoughts. I enjoy being with the girls and telling them my stories. It moved me how quiet and gentle they became when I told "Shadow" after the silliness of "Anansi and Lion." They all shared stories of lost pets, and they taught me several Gaelic songs and games. Children are the same everywhere, and I delight in them all.*

It is for Rosemarie, Kerryann, and Jennifer; for my nephews, Ryan and Dana and their someday children; for my amazing and beautiful daughter, Jamie; and for all the children everywhere that we must keep the stories alive. Without the stories we have no history and no understanding of who we are or who we could be.

REFERENCES

Macleod, Kenneth, and Marjory Kennedy-Fraser. *Songs of the Hebrides*. London: Boosey, 1921.

Smout, T. C. "Highlanders and Lowlanders." In *Insight Guides: Scotland* edited by Brian Bell. Boston: Houghton Mifflin, 1994.

Mary Sarah MacNeil of Ceol Mara.

(L-R) Jennifer, Rosemarie, and Kerryann, the
next generation of storytellers.

✥ Acknowledgments

I would like to acknowledge and thank the following people for their help in making this book such a joy to create:

Glenn Wrightson, George Seto, and Liam Cassidy for the Gaelic;

Frank Dagostino for the Welsh;

Bob Carmody, for the poem, "The Celtic Breeze," which gave me comfort during the lonely times, as well as the title for my book;

Andy Brown, for the musical scores;

Mary Sarah MacNeil, for her hospitality and friendship while I stayed at her bed and breakfast, *Ceol Mara*, on the Isle of Barra;

All the wonderful storytellers on the Isle of Barra, who gave of their time and memories so graciously, and almost always with tea and biscuits;

Robert McNeil, my father, who gave me the pride to be a McNeil, the ability to conquer the challenges necessary to follow a dream, and so much more;

Bonnie McNeil, my mother, who gave me the gift of stories, the ability to believe in the faery world, and so much more; and

Jamie, my amazing and beautiful daughter, who has taught me that family is more than blood.

Introduction

THE CELTS

One cannot consider the faery worlds of Scotland, Wales, and Ireland without considering the Celtic world from which they appeared. They are intertwined throughout their histories, similar in passions that often led to battle as well as romance, fond of rituals and traditions that established or destroyed relationships with nature and other forms of life, and touched by the magic and spirits of transformation and rebirth.

For centuries, the dominant picture of a Celt was of a warrior. Described as gluttons, head hunters, and bloodthirsty barbarians, Celts were often depicted as quarrelsome, boastful, and fearless in battle. The Roman general Julius Caesar described their showmanship and arrogance during chariot warfare, and Diodorus Siculus claimed that, upon acceptance of a one-on-one fight with an opposing warrior, "They loudly recite the deeds of valor of their ancestors and proclaim their own valorous quality, at the same time abusing and making little of their opponent and generally attempting to rob him beforehand of his fighting spirit" (Time-Life Books, p. 65).

As is often the case with historical accounts, these were written by adversaries of the Celts and show a bias from the enemy's point of view. When all the evidence is considered, what is revealed is a complex society of farmers, warriors, and poets, deeply affected by their relationship with the varied forces and forms of nature. Their civilization ranged from the British Isles to the Balkans, Turkey, Italy, Spain, France, and Germany. They were not one society, but many, and their ethnic unity was only in their language. Political structures varied from small tribal chiefdoms to highly centralized states. Druidism, often considered to be common among the Celts, was confined to the northwest. A single, "typical" Celtic religion never existed, but similar myths of sun gods, sky gods, and mother goddesses appear throughout the culture.

The early Celts had no written history, so an accurate portrayal must be created by combining three forms of evidence:

- *Documentary*, including inscriptions on coins, stone inscriptions, and texts from the Greek and Roman contemporaries of the ancient Celts during the Iron Age and throughout the Roman period;

- *Linguistic*, revealed through Celtic names, words in classical texts, surviving Celtic place-names, and the languages that exist today (including Welsh, Breton, Cornish, modern Irish, Scots Gaelic, and Manx); and

- *Archaeological*, which provides a partial picture that identifies patterns only but is free from the prejudices of authors who were adversaries.

TWENTY-FIVE CENTURIES OF CELTS

It is impossible to describe in a few pages the intricate history of the triumphs and tragedies of the Celts. But Simon James, in *The World of the Celts*, and David Bellingham, in *An Introduction to Celtic Mythology*, provide a brief history that will be outlined here, to give readers an idea of the magnitude of the story of the Celts.

The Prehistoric Celt

As early as 1000 B.C. a culture described as "proto-Celtic" lived around the upper Danube. Some archaeologists believe their influence already existed in Bronze Age northern and western Europe. Celtic Britain might date back as far as 1500 B.C., conforming with ancient Irish Celtic myths.

Hallstatt, La Tene, and the Gauls

The earliest writing about the Celts is in Greek literature dated around 500 B.C., and by then they were already settled in parts of Spain and central France. They are now considered to have been part of the Hallstatt culture of the European Iron Age, and excavations have revealed evidence of trade with the classical Mediterranean. Beginning in the fifth century B.C., a new culture developed, named after the archaeological site of La Tene in Switzerland, and ranging from eastern France to Bohemia. The Celts sacked Rome in 390 B.C., and it is then that we first hear them described as *Galli* or *Gauls*, a name given to them by the Romans. The Greeks named them *Keltoi* or *Galatae*; they were attacked by the Celts, perhaps even losing Delphi to them in 279 B.C. During the fifth and fourth centuries B.C., the Celts spread to the British Isles, and by the third century B.C., "the Celtic world consisted of a shifting mosaic of autonomous tribes and states stretching from Ireland to Hungary, with isolated pockets and partly Celtic populations from Portugal to Turkey" (James, p. 12).

Conquest of the Celts, Third Century B.C.–Fifth Century A.D.

From the third to the first centuries B.C., the Celtic worlds began to come under pressure of the Germans. The conquest of Gaul by Rome in the 50s B.C. was the greatest blow, and by the new millennium, only the British Isles were still dominated by Celts. That, too, changed quickly, with Romans invading southeastern Britain in A.D. 43 and conquering as far as the Scottish Highlands by the early 80s. The north, however, remained undefeated, and Ireland escaped undisturbed until the later fourth and fifth centuries. After Rome fell in the fifth century A.D. and the old Celtic lands came under Germanic rule, even the name of Gaul disappeared, replaced by *France*, an adaptation of the name of the Germanic tribe, Franks.

Celtic Revival and Destruction, Sixth–Nineteenth Centuries A.D.

Because Britain was never as thoroughly Romanized as Gaul, the Celtic language and social structure continued to flourish in the west and north of Britain. In the sixth century there appeared new British and Welsh kingdoms, La Tene style art made a comeback, and western Britons crossed the channel to establish Brittany. Meanwhile, Ireland was quickly becoming one of the great centers of Christianity, and monks began establishing famous monasteries, such as Iona on the west coast of Scotland. Irish sea-rovers, known as *Scotti*, founded a kingdom in western Caledonia, later to become known as Scotland.

At the end of the eighth century Vikings appeared, and the Celtic revival ended. The Norsemen ravaged Europe and invaded Ireland, beginning a long history of foreign intervention there. The disintegration of the Celtic world now included the British Isles. James succinctly describes the next 800 years of change:

The story of the Celts in the later Middle Ages is one of gradual absorption and partial assimilation. Wales lost her independence in the thirteenth century, by which time the Celtic identity of Cornwall was being rapidly eroded. Brittany was subsumed within France in 1532. Ireland only fell fully under English rule during the reign of Elizabeth I. Her death in 1603 also began the final unification of England with Scotland; the two countries were formally unified in 1707. The Gaelic-speaking clan society of Scotland's Highlands and Islands was effectively destroyed after the rebellion of 1745. Ireland was also incorporated into the United Kingdom, in 1801. (p. 13)

The Highland Clearances, Nineteenth Century A.D.

Then came the horrors of the Highland Clearances. During the late eighteenth and early nineteenth centuries, Scottish landlords systematically replaced people with the more economically profitable sheep in an effort to increase the profit from their lands. Lowland shepherds and their stock displaced the crofters and their cattle, and tenants were evicted with true ruthlessness. David Craig recounts horrific stories in *On the Crofters' Trail: In Search of the Clearance Highlanders*. Houses were unroofed to force out the tenants, people were tied up with ropes and loaded into small boats, and the year 1814 became know as *Bliadhna an Losgaidh*, the Year of the Burnings. One particularly poignant story tells of Jane Anderson, who "was lured out by the ground officers with a story about her cow having strayed into the corn—she left her child and went after the animal—when she came back the child was outside on the ground and the thatch was burning." Thousands of starving families were left homeless. The Potato Famine of the 1840s in Ireland also resulted in a horrific loss of life. Approximately one million people died of starvation when blight destroyed the main food source for the Irish farmers. For many, the combination of agricultural failure at home and the lure of new opportunities overseas led to a mass migration into the expanding countries of Canada, Australia, and the United States.

The Modern Celt

It is an admirable testimony to the endurance of the Celtic culture that while its language was being actively suppressed during the nineteenth and twentieth centuries, several simultaneous archaeological rediscoveries of the past contributed to a national self-pride in modern Celtic Europe. Irish statehood was established in 1921, and there are vigorous nationalist movements in Wales, Scotland, and Brittany even today. The development of Welsh and Gaelic television has contributed to the fact that Celtic languages are experiencing a resurgence, and people of Celtic ancestry are embracing and promoting knowledge of their complex and dramatic history. The popularity of Irish dancing, Celtic art, and movies depicting legendary Scottish heroes has increased the awareness of the Celts and their influence on modern society. A passion for discovering one's family history and tracing the genealogical roots to the earliest aboriginal beginnings has led people to claim their Celtic history with pride. As Tadhg MacCrossan states in his pamphlet, "The Truth About the Druids," "As long as there are people who remember their Celtic heritage and its contributions to modern culture and civilization, the legends, folk-tales, and myths of the Celtic peoples, there will be those who dream about the ancient Celtic magic."

CELTIC FOLKLORE AND BELIEFS

Throughout all the centuries of movement and change among the Celts, stories were told in Ireland, Scotland, and Wales, stories of heroes and transformation and earth goddesses. It is again, through a combination of sources, that we must rediscover the myths, legends, and faery tales of the British Celt. It was not until the eighth century A.D. that the oral tales were written down, and then by Irish monks who had a bias of their own as the Christian, Celtic, and classical civilizations mingled, creating what is now known as the Insular culture. The earliest existing collection is *Lebor na hUidre* (*The Book of the Dun Cow*), a Christianized version of the old stories about the Irish hero Cu Chulainn. His story was written down in the twelfth century A.D. by Maelmuri, and was based on a lost earlier manuscript of the seventh century written on cowhide by St. Ciaran. The *Mabinogion*, a collection of eleven Welsh tales from manuscripts of the fourteenth century, provides the basis for much of the best-known British mythology.

For the most part, information about and myths of the ancient Celts were passed on orally by trained professionals. Among the earliest Celts, these were the druids, and, later, bards and seers. Druids were responsible not only for the recitation of epic poems and histories but also for divination, prophecy, supervision of religious activities, and memorization of long and complex law codes. They were "the supreme guardians of the sacred lore" and also predicted the best times for battles, harvests, and ceremonies of inauguration (Wood, p. 104). Both the Greek author Strabo and the Roman general Julius Caesar provide long accounts of the role of the druids and the great respect in which they were held by their followers.

Diodorus of Sicily wrote in the first century B.C. that the bards "converse with few words and in riddles, mainly using obscure hints to refer to things and saying one word when they mean another; and they tend to use superlatives to boost their own achievements and put down those of other[s]" (Bellingham, p. 48). In the fourth century A.D., the Roman writer Ammianus Marcellinus stated, "The bards celebrated the brave deeds of famous men in epic verse to the accompaniment of the sweet strains of the lyre." Joy Chant, in *The High Kings,* describes the bard as "the keeper of the soul of the people, a 'poet-priest' " (p. 16).

Druids were also the interpreters of natural phenomena and the intermediaries between the mortal world and the Otherworld. They used nature's own boundaries, such as trees or the banks of a lake, to separate sacred space from the human world, believing that divinity resided in all corners of the natural world. The boundaries flowed and changed, and humans could cross over at their own risk into the Otherworld, where they would find supernatural beings, as well as humans who had died. An ancient Irish legend tells of Dechtire, daughter of a druid mortal and a goddess. She was to marry Sualtaim Mac Roth, an Ulster chieftain, but at her wedding feast she drank a fly that landed in her cup. She fell into a deep sleep and woke in the Otherworld, where she became the lover of the god Lugh Lamhfada and gave birth to a boy, Setanta. She returned to Ulster, Sualtaim accepted her child as his own, and the boy was renamed Cu Chulainn, one of the greatest and most tragic of Irish heroes.

At certain times of seasonal change, however, the boundaries disappeared altogether. The inhabitants of the Otherworld emerged from the pre-Celtic barrows and other burial sites and roamed among the humans in their world. Traditionally, this occurred during the agricultural cycles of *Imbolg* or *Imbolc* (February 1), meaning "Sheep's Milk," which marked the beginning of spring and the birth of livestock; *Beltaine* (May 1), or "Great Fire," which celebrated the beginning of summer; *Lughnasa* (August 1), the feast of the god Lugh to honor the harvest; and *Samhain* (November 1), or "End of Summer." Many of these traditions were absorbed and transformed by the Christians. For instance, the *Samhain* Festival, held on the evening of October 31 and into the following day was changed to Hallowe'en followed by All Saints Day or All Hallows in an effort to forget the pagan tradition that believed the dead walked among the living on that day.

Forest groves were especially hallowed, and a form of the word *nemeton,* meaning sacred grove, is found throughout the world of Celtic languages. Votive offerings and cult statues have been found in the forest groves near Perthshire, Scotland, and at many other sites. The Celtic deity associated with the woods was *Cernunnos,* "Horned Sacred One," a lord of the animals with deer-like antlers. He was believed to be associated with the abundance of nature and with masculine potency. Often depicted as a stag, his shedding and growing of antlers symbolized renewal and regeneration.

Trees also represented the seasonal cycles. With their branches reaching up toward the mysteries of the heavens and their roots pushing down toward the mysteries of the earth, they were considered to be associated with the all-important themes of death, rebirth, growth, and longevity of life. Legends such as that of Aillinn present this image of eternal life through the supernatural power of trees. Aillinn was granddaughter of the king of Leinster, and Baile was heir to the kingdom of Ulster. Their love for each other was prohibited by the deadly enmity of Leinster and Ulster, and both Baile and Aillinn died from their broken hearts. A yew tree grew from the grave of Baile at Traigh mBaile, and an apple tree grew over Aillinn's grave. The poets of Ulster and Leinster cut branches from the trees and carved the tragic story on wands made from the branches. According to legend, 200 years later the wands were taken to Tech Screpta, the library at Tara. As they were placed side by side for the first time, they sprang together and could not be separated.

Bodies of water held great significance for the Celts as being homes to gods and goddesses, or shape-shifters. Offerings such as weapons were often thrown into sacred lakes to attract the favor of the gods. Many relics of high-quality metalwork have been found in Llyn Cerrig Bach on Anglesey, Wales, and one can easily understand the origins of the story of King Arthur commanding Bedivere to throw his sword Excalibur to the Lady of the Lake. Cauldrons were offered to water divinities, and the "Cauldron of Rebirth," which restored the dead to life in the medieval Welsh *Mabinogi*, is said to have emerged from a lake.

Wells were also believed to have significant powers, such as the one guarded by the hag in "Niall of the Nine Hostages" in this collection. Another story tells of the power of Segais's Well, believed to be the source of the inspiration of knowledge. Boann, whose name meant "she of the white cattle," refused to accept the taboo that allowed only four people to visit the well, and she walked defiantly around it in a left-hand circle. The waters of the well rose up and drowned her, and it is the course of those waters that forms the river, now known as the Boyne, named for the goddess.

Springs were believed to have curative powers. The sanctuary of the goddess Sulis Minerva at the ancient springs of Bath, England, continues to be a site for pilgrims seeking miracles. Rivers, a symbol of the source of life, often had a guardian goddess. Their names are still used today, for example for the Welsh rivers of Dyfrdonwy and Trydonwy. These names are both derived from Donwy, or Don, the Welsh equivalent of Danu, the "mother goddess." In England the rivers Don in Durham and Yorkshire are named after her.

Celtic heroes were believed to meet at the ford of a river for combat, hoping they would not encounter the "Washer at the Ford," a faery woman who washed the clothes of those destined to die that day. Aquatic animals were often depicted as symbols of the connection between the Otherworld and the world of the mortals, thus leading to the Scottish stories of selkies, who were seals in the water and human on land, and kelpies, who appeared on earth as black horses but dragged their mortal prey to a watery grave in the loch.

Other animals representing the metamorphosis motif frequently appear in Celtic tales and art, again relating to the fluid boundaries between the supernatural and the natural. An Irish myth tells of the hero Oengus taking on the form of a swan during the feast of *Samhain,* and "The Children of Lir," one of the great stories of sorrow from Ireland, concerns the transformation of the king's sons and daughters into swans. Battle goddesses assumed the form of crows and ravens, beautiful women, or hags. The divine wife of the Irish hero Fionn first appears to her husband as a fawn. In one of the four branches, or tales, from the *Mabinogi,* a magical woman takes the form of a mouse to torment heroes. In another Welsh legend, the magicians Gwydion and Math create a beautiful woman from flowers, but when she proves unfaithful to her husband, Lleu, she is turned into an owl, representing the evil forces of darkness. The Scottish story of young *Tam Lin* relates how a faery queen changes one of her knights into many horrifying and deadly animal shapes to frighten away his mortal lover.

All of these changes are thought to indicate a belief in regeneration and afterlife, a never-ending circle that was later displayed in the well-known design of the Celtic knot, "an unbroken path without beginning or end" (Wood, p. 79). Although the knot for the Irish scribes was a symbol of "the boundlessness of God and the infinite diversity of his creation" (Wood, p. 79), its origins were in the plait motifs of the La Tene culture, from 500 B.C. until the first centuries A.D., and it was often decorated with the magical beasts and representations of nature so important to Celtic stories.

Another belief among the Celts that appeared in their stories is the importance of replication in threes. Wood theorizes in her book that perhaps it symbolized the continuity of time, such as past, present, and future, or the parts of the universe, such as earth, the heavens, and the underworld. Good-luck charms of three little figures, called *genii cuculatti,* each wearing cloaks, have been found in an area near Hadrian's wall in Britain, and date back to the first century A.D. The tradition is frequently used as a narrative device, wherein heroes and heroines face tragedy twice and prevail the third time.

Perhaps more than anything else, warriorhood and battle were essential to Celtic society. The Greek historian Strabo (64 B.C.–A.D. 21) declared Celts to be "war mad," and Welsh narratives described heroes that "fought together every May Day until the end of time for the hand of a beautiful woman." The names of the Celtic warriors live on through time and across continents: Cu Chulainn of Ireland; Pryderi of Wales; the Fian Warriors of Ireland and Scotland, "who are said to be waiting in a cavern until the day comes when all Gaeldom shall rise against its oppressors" (Douglas, p. 159); and, of course, King Arthur of Britain, whose legendary image far surpasses the warchief he may have been. These were the stories and epics told by the bards, amazing in their length and complexity. They were legends of fact and fiction, and they were the creations of a society whose imagination knew no limits.

THE OTHERWORLD

> *The ground appeared to open, and they were passing very rapidly under the earth. . . . "Here we are, Jenny," said he, "there is yet a tear of sorrow on your eyelids, and no human tears can enter our homes, let me wipe them away." Again Jenny's eyes were brushed with the small leaves as before, and, lo! before her was such a country as she had never seen previously. Hill and valley were covered with flowers, strangely varied in colour, but combining into a most harmonious whole; so that the region appeared sown with gems which glittered in a light as brilliant as that of the summer sun, yet as mild as the moonlight. There were rivers clearer than any water she had ever seen on the granite hills, and waterfalls and fountains; while everywhere ladies and gentlemen dressed in green and gold were walking, or sporting, or reposing on banks of flowers, singing songs or telling stories. Oh! it was a beautiful world.* ("The Fairy Widower," in *Popular Romances of the West of England*, by Roget Hunt)

The concept of the Otherworld was central to the belief system of the ancient Celts, and we see it repeatedly portrayed as the land of dreams. It is mysterious, magical, eternal, and more than a bit frightening. Anything and everything is possible in the Otherworld, but only if the rules are followed. There are very definite rules, established by the faery and spiritual inhabitants, and the betrayal of those rules is often the theme of the stories about mortals who wander into this mystical land. Time is altogether different, and a human who is granted "a year and a day"

to play with the faery piper, or dance with the wee folk, or search for a lost lover, is often not seen again for a hundred years, if at all. There is no death, illness, or old age, only youth and romance.

There are striking similarities between the Otherworld of the supernatural and the real world of the ancient Celt. The Otherworld is often depicted as being divided into kingdoms under different faery kings and queens, much like the high kings and chiefs of the British Isles. There are feasts, games, loves lost and won, battles, riddles to be guessed, and adventures to be followed. There are some emotions, such as jealousy which often leads to a desire for revenge, and there is sadness, especially among faery women who love a mortal they cannot have.

Gods, faeries, demons, and spirits all have their place in the Otherworld, but humans must live in the limited world of mortals.

> *"Where did you come from, woman?"*
>
> *"From Tir Na mBeo, the Lands of the Living,"* she replied, *"and not of your world, for there you will find no men looking for a fight, and no one dies. We feast without servants, and bear no grudges. See there,"* the woman pointed to a barrow on the ridge. *"That is where we live, and some call us the fairy hill folk."* (Anonymous Irish author of the eighth century, in Bellingham, p. 57)

THE FAERY FOLK

Frequently appearing in this Otherworld are the *Tuatha De Danann*, the people of the goddess Dana. These are the descendants of a majestic race who inhabited Ireland in ancient times but were defeated by the Milesians, ancestors of the Irish people. Those who refused to give up their sacred island became invisible and took refuge under the hills or beneath the waters. Others retreated to *Tir nan Og*, the Land of the Ever Young, "where the grass was always green and fruit and flowers could be picked together, where feasting, music, love, hunting and joyous fighting went on all day and death made no entry, for if in the fights men were wounded and killed one day they came to life again none the worse the next" (Briggs, p. 400). Originally gigantic, and well known for their beauty and magical powers, they diminished in importance, and size, with the increasing popularity of Christianity. They became known as *daoine sidhe*, the faery folk, but, for safety's sake, were given other names such as the "good people," "wee folks," "men of peace," or "the honest folk." So ingrained are they in the folk history of Ireland that even St. Patrick is said to have communicated with *Scothniamh*, a faery woman described as "a lone woman robed in mantle of green, a smock of soft silk being next her skin, and on her forehead a glittering plate of yellow gold" (Evans-Wentz, p. 287).

The concept of faeries as the descendants of supernatural mortals is just one of the many theories of their origin. In Evans-Wentz's book, *The Fairy Faith in Celtic Countries*, he quotes the opinions of people he interviewed in the British Isles in the first decade of the twentieth century. Many of them held the belief that faeries were fallen angels, such as in this explanation from ninety-two-year-old Roderick Macneill, as spoken to the writer J. F. Campbell:

> *The Proud Angel fomented a rebellion among the angels of heaven, where he had been a leading light. He declared that he would go and found a kingdom for himself. When going out at the door of heaven the Proud Angel brought prickly lightning and biting lightning out of the doorstep with his heels. Many angels followed him—so many that at last the Son called out, "Father! Father, the city is being emptied!" whereupon the Father ordered that the gates of heaven and the gates of hell should be closed. This was instantly done. And those who were in were in, and those who were out were out; while the hosts who had left heaven and had not reached hell flew into the holes of the earth, like the stormy petrels. These are the Fairy Folk—ever since doomed to live under the ground, and only allowed to emerge where and when the King permits.* (Evans-Wentz, p. 85)

Dr. Alexander Carmichael translated the following from the Gaelic recited by Ann Macneill of Barra in 1865, and Angus Macleod of Harris, in 1877:

> *There is no growth nor increase, no death nor withering upon the fairies. Seed unfortunate they! They went away from the Paradise with the One of the Great Pride. When the Father commanded the doors closed down and up, the intermediate fairies had no alternative but to leap into the holes of the earth, where they are, and where they will be.* (Evans-Wentz, p. 115)

These quotes concerning this theory of faeries as fallen angels clearly exemplify a modern Christian's attempt to explain the supernatural folklore he or she so desperately wishes to understand. But there are other theories, and it is the intertwining of them all that leads to the stories and traditions that have been passed on from ancient bards to modern storytellers.

One idea that is frequently expressed in the folklore of Scotland is that faeries are spirits. Ninety-four-year-old John Campbell of the Isle of Barra gave the following testimony to Walter Yeeling Evans-Wentz:

> The general belief of the people here during my father's lifetime was that the fairies were more of the nature of spirits than of men made of flesh and blood, but that they so appeared to the naked eye that no difference could be marked in their forms from that of any human being, except that they were more diminutive. (Evans-Wentz, p. 104)

Marian MacLean of Barra described the differences between faeries, who appear in the shape of human beings, and hosts, or *sluagh*, who are spirits of the dead:

> Generally, the fairies are to be seen after or about sunset, and walk on the ground as we do, whereas the hosts travel in the air above places inhabited by people. The hosts used to go after the fall of night, and more particularly about midnight. You'd hear them going in fine weather against a wind like a covey of birds. And they were in the habit of lifting men in South Uist, for the hosts need men to help in shooting their javelins from their bows against women in the action of milking cows, or against any person working at night in a house over which they pass. And I have heard of good sensible men whom the hosts took, shooting a horse or cow in place of the person ordered to be shot. (Evans-Wentz, p. 108)

Katharine Briggs, in her well-known *Encyclopedia of Fairies*, describes the various classes of the dead:

> The Sluagh or fairy Hosts are the evil dead, according to Highland belief. Finvarra's following in Ireland seem to comprise the dead who have recently died as well as the ancient dead; but they are almost as sinister as the Sluagh. In Cornwall the Small People are the souls of the heathen dead, who died before Christianity and were not good enough for Heaven nor bad enough for Hell, and therefore lingered on, gradually shrinking until they became as small as ants, and disappeared altogether out of the world. . . . In Cornwall and Devon too the souls of unchristened babies were called Piskies, and appeared at twilight in the form of little white

moths. In Wales the belief in the fairies as the dead does not seem to have been so common. They were often described as a race of "beings half-way between something material and spiritual, who were rarely seen," or "a real race of invisible or spiritual beings living in an invisible world of their own." (Briggs, pp. 318–19)

Evans-Wentz described several theories of the origin of faeries, based on his interviews with people in Ireland, the Highlands and Islands of Scotland, Wales, the Isle of Man, Cornwall, and Brittany. The Naturalistic Theory holds that spirits, gods, and faeries were created as "attempts to explain or to rationalize natural phenomena" (p. xxix). The Druid Theory alleges that "the folk memory of the Druids and their magical practices is alone responsible for the Fairy-Faith" (p. xxxi). The Mythological Theory claims that faeries "are the diminished figures of the old pagan divinities of the early Celts" (p. xxxii), and the Pygmy Theory is based on a folk memory of an actual Pygmy race that was "driven into mountain fastnesses and into the most inaccessible places, where a few of them may have survived until comparatively historical times" (p. xxx). It is probably this last theory that "logically" accounts for the practices of kidnapping healthy babies and leaving behind weakened children, and of milking cows until they were dry under cover of night's darkness.

ARE FAERIES REAL?

Yes. And no.

There is no conclusive proof or disproof of the existence of Celtic faeries, any more than there is one overall description of their appearance. But what can be stated is that the bards and the druids and the seers believed in the faery world because they allowed themselves to. Their lives were free of all the technological, mechanical, and physical encumbrances that separate mortals today from the mystical. The Celts lived close to the earth, and they listened to it. They were touched daily by the powers and phenomena of nature, and, rather than trying to control it by explaining it away in terms of degrees of barometric pressure or the gravitational pull of the moon, they were awed and humbled by how nature controlled them. They gave honor and recognition to the forces of sky and earth and water; they told stories about those forces; and they did not "logically" prohibit themselves from knowing the magical, powerful, inexplicable inhabitants of those worlds. You have only to imagine a world without electricity, neighborhoods, or paper, and then you can begin to understand the power of the combination of knowledge based on experience and spirituality based on imagination that created the faery world. As Leslie Shepard states in *The Fairy-Faith in Celtic Countries,* "Insulated in cities by bricks and concrete, pampered by science and confused by the impatient and intricate demands of the practical world, (civilized man) has become separated from that great stream of bright legend and myth that is the mystery and art of folk cultures; his mystical vision has atrophied" (foreword).

But W. Y. Evans-Wentz, a Ph.D. in comparative religion, an author, and an anthropologist, said it best in *The Fairy-Faith in Celtic Countries:*

> *Not only has (the Celtic peasant) the will to believe, but he has the right to believe; because his belief is not a matter of being educated and reasoning logically, nor a matter of faith and theology—it is a fact of his own individual experiences, as he will tell you. Such peasant seers have frequently argued with me to the effect that "One does not have to be educated in order to see fairies." (p. xxxiv)*

REFERENCES

Bellingham, David. *An Introduction to Celtic Mythology.* Secaucus, NJ: Chartwell Books, 1990.

Briggs, Katharine. *An Encyclopedia of Fairies: Hobgoblins, Brownies, Bogies, and Other Supernatural Creatures.* New York: Pantheon Books, 1976.

Chant, Joy. *The High Kings: Arthur's Celtic Ancestors.* New York: Bantam Books, 1983.

Craig, David. *On the Crofters' Trail: In Search of the Clearance Highlanders.* London: Cape, 1990.

Douglas, Ronald Macdonald. *Scottish Lore and Folklore.* New York: Beekman House, 1982.

Evans-Wentz, W. Y. *The Fairy-Faith in Celtic Countries.* New York: Carol Publishing, 1990.

Hunt, Roget. *Popular Romances of the West of England; or, The Drolls, Traditions, and Superstitions of Old Cornwall.* London: John Camden Hotten, 1871.

James, Simon. *The World of the Celts.* London: Thames & Hudson, 1993.

MacCrossan, Tadhg. "The Truth About the Druids." Pamphlet.

Shepard, Leslie. "Foreword." In *The Fairy Faith in Celtic Countries,* by W. Y. Evans-Wentz. New York: Carol Publishing, 1990.

Time-Life Books. *Celts: Europe's People of Iron.* Alexandria, VA: Time-Life Books, 1994.

Wood, Juliette. *The Celts: Life, Myth, and Art.* New York: Stewart, Tabori & Chang, 1998.

✸ The Songs of the Hebrides

Nothing can equal the delicious sadness of the Celtic melodies;
like emanations from above they fall, drop by drop, upon the
soul, and pass through it like the memories of another world.
Kennedy-Fraser and Macleod, p. xv

Like many ancient people, the Celts celebrated the joys and sorrows of life through their music as well as their stories. Occasionally, the two oral arts combined into epic ballads, which related fantastic episodes of heroes, heroines, and supernatural beings. Many of these ballads live on today, due to the preservation efforts of folklorists and anthropologists such as Marjory Kennedy-Fraser and Kenneth Macleod.

Beginning in the summer of 1905, Kennedy-Fraser traveled to the Hebrides to record the songs of the islanders. Macleod provided the Gaelic and English, and the result is a three-volume set titled *Songs of the Hebrides*, published in 1909. The collection is a unique and invaluable celebration of the ballads, labor songs, chants, and mouth music of a people whose hearts beat to the songs of the sea and the moor. Almost every song is accompanied by a story, for the two are often intertwined and inseparable. Notes about pronunciations, history, and musical theory are included, adding greatly to the value for musicians, storytellers, folklorists, and historians.

Equally as valuable as the songs are the descriptions by Kennedy-Fraser and Macleod of the people they encountered and the homes they visited. They reveal a civilization that has vanished with the progress brought about by the introduction of electricity, a civilization that always put an extra amount into the porridge for the stranger that might be visiting and that listened to the land and the sea to find the music.

Following are two of their recollections:

Making our way over slippery rocks, we at last struck a pathway
(the only road in the island, and that but recently made), and
here and there, as though dropped at random on the bare rock,
or nestling into the hillside, we came upon long, oval huts, built
of undressed stone, innocent of cement or lime, and thatched
with bracken, fastened by ropes of heather. Silent figures moved
quietly about in the dim, fading light, now a man, now an old

woman, now a dog, all with the characteristic quiet gait of the Western Highlander, giving a dreamy character to the whole picture, a dreaminess which did not vanish, I found, even in bright sunlight, for when I woke next morning and looked from my window out on to the sea from the house on the rock, I seemed to be on an enchanted island. (p. xvii)

On moonlight nights, if the tide be suitable, the men folk of the little isle cross over to Uist, each going his own way according to the errand he is on, and some time before midnight they all form again in the headland house overlooking the ford. A youth is placed at the western window to watch for the appearing of certain reefs above water—the rider's reef, if ponies are at hand, the footman's otherwise; the rest of the company are in the humour for a ceilidh, and if wit and humour, tales old and new, ballads of the brave long ago and satires on the latest wedding or the latest heresy hunt, can make a ceilidh, then here is the best in the Outer Isles—the ceilidh which never yawns. Time and tide are left waiting outside, and the reefs become dry, and wet again, ere the men rise to go; and as the last of them rides or wades across the ford, one feels that here is a world, in the world, of which London is not the centre, and gold not the god, and in which a man has time to remember that he is soul as well as flesh. (p. xxxviii)

I have included several of the songs from *Songs of the Hebrides* that complement or enhance the interpretation of my retelling of Celtic stories. Some are directly related, such as "Christ Child's Lullaby." Others are merely about the same subject, such as "The Skye Water Kelpie's Lullaby," and others interpret the mood, such as "Sea Sorrow" and "The Wind on the Moor." I have included only the basic tunes, but *Songs of the Hebrides* offers the full piano accompaniment. I have also transcribed only the English, but Macleod offers the Gaelic as well, along with basic guidelines for the pronunciation of this very difficult language.

It is important to note that many of the songs include a frequently repeated phrase that has no literal translation into English but is rewritten into words that sound closest to how the Gaelic is pronounced. These chants are part of the tradition of mouth music and, as Kennedy-Fraser explains:

In their happy arrangements of beautiful vowel sounds and syllables which at times have no meaning save a musical one, the Celtic folk are artistically right. For there is no reason why vocal music should not, in common with instrumental music, express emotion in purely musical terms. . . . [T]he singer should attempt the singing of them, since much of the intended purely musical effect of such songs is lost if words with a definite meaning are used through-out. It is precisely because the Isles folk are so musical that they do not want definite literal sense to unduly deaden the more highly emotional effect of pure sound.

The songs are unusual and sometimes difficult. They are included in this book because they are unique to the Hebrides, very representative of the spirit of these people who were undaunted by the forces that could as easily bring them death as life: the wind, the mist, and above all, the sea. The Isles are shrouded in mystery and charm. From craggy shores to endless moors, from standing stones left behind by ancient civilizations to shipwrecks that haunt the memories of those left behind, you cannot escape the possibility of a story and a song.

REFERENCES

Kennedy-Fraser, Marjory, and Kenneth Macleod. *Songs of the Hebrides*. New York: Boosey, 1921.

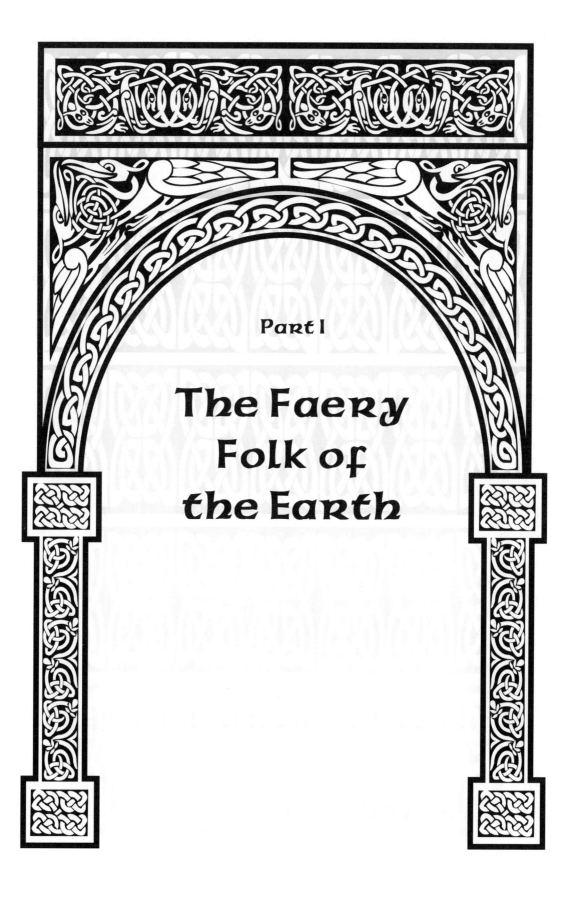

Part I

The Faery Folk of the Earth

The Changeling Child

INTRODUCTION

T he story "The Changeling Child" was told to me by Kirsty MacKay, the mother of the priest on the Isle of Barra. She is a clever woman in her mid-eighties, crippled and hunched over with osteoporosis but strong with memories and humor. She was a teacher sixty years ago in the highlands, and she used stories in her classroom. She was pleased to remember them for me and insisted her son type them out before I heard them. I returned to his home next to the Catholic church the following evening, and she presented me with three stories, which she read aloud so I could record her voice as well as the words. She regretted the imperfections of translating from Gaelic into English. "You need to have the Gaelic to truly understand these stories," she said, more than once.

Mrs. MacKay lives on South Uist, an island that stretches for miles with flat bogs and peat. "This island [the Isle of Barra] makes me nervous, it has so many hills," she told me. "I shall be glad to go back home."

I will be forever grateful to serendipity that arranged for this generous and hospitable woman to be visiting the home of her son while I was visiting the home of my ancestors.

The Changeling Child

Leanamh Tacharan[1]

There was once a farmer, Aonghas Mor, who lived with his wife, Mairead, and baby son, Aonghas Beag. Their croft was a home and farm small in size but large with the love they felt for each other.

Now, Aonghas Mor was often away from the croft, buying and selling cows at the market. While he was gone, Mairead helped time pass by tending to her knitting, cooking, and, best of all, the wee *bairn*,[2] Aonghas Beag. She sang softly to her son about the sea and the wind. She rocked him in his cradle and told him the stories of faeries that her mother had told to her. And when she missed Aonghas Mor more than she thought she could bear, she would hold her son in her arms and dance in the heather that was the carpet of the moors.

One summer day, Aonghas Mor said good-bye and left to take a cow and her calf to market. After a lingering farewell, Mairead finished her chores of cleaning the wee cottage. She fed Aonghas Beag and bathed him and then decided, it being a day of sunshine and gentle winds, she would sit outside and knit with the *bairn*, her baby, beside her in his cradle. So out they went, and as Mairead lifted the cradle she was careful not to lose the sprig of rowan tree that always hung from the hood of the cradle for protection against the faeries.

There they sat, Mairead knitting a wee jacket for her son, and her son laughing in his cradle and looking up at his mother, his green eyes dancing in the light.

While they sat there, a stranger came among them, a weary old man trudging down the road. Dressed in rags and tatters he was, and a scraggly white beard frosted his tired face.

"*Latha math dhuibh*.[3] Good day to you, old man," said Mairead.

---

1. LYEN-uv TAKH-uh-run
2. bayrn
3. lah mah GOO-iv; Good day to you.

"*Latha math dhuibh fhein.*[4] Good day to you, Mairead," he replied.

"And how is it that you know my name when I do not know yours?"

"I know of many things that are and are not, in this world and in others."

"What else do you know besides my name?"

The stranger smiled. "I know that I have come a long way on a hot day, and I know that I am thirsty. I should be very grateful for a drink of water, please."

"A drink you shall have, old man, and better than water," said Mairead. She went into the house and returned with a large glass of milk, freshly taken from the cow that morning. The stranger drank it all, then wiped his mouth with a ragged sleeve.

"*Tapadh leibh.*[5] Thank you, kindly. And now I shall tell this that I know." The old man reached into a pocket inside his worn coat and brought out something wrapped tightly in his fist. "I know that this will help you in desperate times," he said, wrapping both of his hands around one of Mairead's and dropping the object, small and light, in her hand. "Keep it with you always. Good-bye," said the stranger as he walked away, not quite as stooped or tired as when he had appeared.

Mairead opened her hand, and what was there but a rusty old nail! Mairead laughed, for she had been thinking of a gift of golden coins or fertile seeds. She put the nail in the pocket of her apron and thought no more about it.

When the long shadows of the afternoon began to appear, Mairead returned Aonghas Beag and his cradle to the cottage. The boy slept soundly as she began her work of lighting the fire for cooking the evening meal.

Suddenly there was a great commotion outside. The red cow was lowing, the speckled hens were cackling and clucking, and the rooster was crowing like a banshee.

"What is all that about?" thought Mairead, and she ran outside. What she found was strange indeed. The red cow was lazily chewing her cud, her eyes closed. The little speckled hens and the rooster were sound asleep, their beaks tucked under their wings.

"I don't understand," said Mairead, standing there in the peace and quiet of the byre. "There was all that noise, now nothing. The animals aren't even awake. It's as if they were bewitched by *sithichean.*[6]"

---

4. lah mah GOO-iv hayn; Good day to you. (reply)
5. TAH-puh lev
6. SHEE-uh-khun; faeries

And as soon as she said that word—faeries—Mairead thought of her wee *bairn*, left by himself in the cottage. With no breath in her mouth, she ran back toward the house.

The first thing she saw was the sprig of rowan lying on the ground just outside the front door where it must have dropped when she carried the cradle inside. The second thing she saw was the cradle rocking to and fro, back and forth, as if someone had just brushed against it. And the third thing she saw was a curtain fluttering at the open window—but there was no wind.

Mairead ran to the cradle. Aonghas Beag was gone. But there was a *leanamh tacharan*, a changeling child, an old, wizened, and unearthly-looking creature that girned and grumbled, staring at her with eyes darker than burning peat.

"Tis the faery folk," Mairead whispered. "The faeries have taken my son and left me one of their own in his place." She stood there, next to the cradle that held the changeling child, and thought of her own, with eyes the color of the fern. "Ach, I cannot bear it."

Mairead would search for Aonghas Beag from the islands to the highlands, but where to begin? Where would the faeries take her child? "I know who can tell me!" Mairead put a white shawl about her, and out the door she went, after attending to the *tacharan* as well as she could but hearing only its whines and moans for all her care.

Mairead knew of an old woman who lived alone on the moors and was known for her healing ways and for her wisdom about *sithichean*. It was to her that Mairead went, and it was to her she told the story of the rowan and the *tacharan* and the missing *bairn*, more precious to her than life itself.

The old woman listened with never a question, her eyes gazing toward the sea. When Mairead was finished, finally giving in to the tears that replaced the words, the wise woman spoke.

"You are right, Mairead. The faeries have taken your son, and the faeries must be the ones to give him back to you. Are you brave of heart?"

"Aye, that I am. For my son, I am brave like the wee sparrow that dives at the eagle to save her nest."

"Then here is what you must do. Tonight, at midnight, you must be at the knoll that is covered with neither gorse nor heather. When the moon is neither bright nor dark, stamp three times, and the faery folk will open their world to you. But what you will find there, I do not know, for no one has ever been to that world and returned to tell what she saw. Now, go. And be brave, Mairead. Be brave of heart."

Her soul heavy with sorrow, and her thoughts heavy with questions, Mairead walked slowly home. How would she ever find a knoll "that is covered with neither gorse nor heather"? And how could the moon be "neither bright nor dark"? Above all, she wondered if she would ever sleep again beside her own dear Aonghas Mor, with their son asleep in his cradle beside them.

When Mairead returned to the cottage, she found the *tacharan* still in the cradle, and no matter what she did to make him comfortable, he only howled and screamed and whined and moaned, his nut-brown face twisted in anger. Finally, she left him and sat by the fire, her hands tightly folded in her lap, her eyes closed on memories of husband and child.

The evening passed. In the dark hour before midnight, Mairead threw her white shawl over her head and shoulders again and began her search for *sithean*,[7] the faery knoll. She did not know where to look but let the brave and broken heart of a grieving mother guide her feet. And find it she did, far out in the moors. A knoll that was covered with neither gorse nor heather, but stones that shone through the darkness.

There she stood, her feet firmly on the rocks, her shawl draped about her like a cloak of moonlight, and her eyes lifted to the stars. A wee sparrow looking for an eagle, she waited until the moon was covered by the shadow of an eclipse, so that it was neither bright nor dark.

Immediately, Mairead stamped three times.

"Who's there?" crackled a voice from beneath the earth.

"A mortal woman."

"What do you want?"

"I want to come inside."

Mairead heard shrieks of laughter. "It is not often that a mortal wants in here," croaked the voice, "for anyone who comes in to our world does not go out the same. But come in, and say farewell to all you have known and loved."

Before she could breathe her next breath, Mairead found herself standing inside the knoll. There was no way in or out that she had seen, only a feeling of cold dampness that wrapped itself about her and pulled her down—down—down, into a world that was both dream and nightmare.

Dark shadows flitted among the dim light of torches. Sharp fingers pinched her skin and pulled her hair. Whispers played about her ears, wings beat the air, and she could hear the creatures of the earth wiggling and crawling and scrabbling their way toward her.

---

7. SHEE-hun

Mairead began to walk down a path that was more hoped for than seen. She pushed aside vines that slapped her face, her feet slipping on moss and moldy leaves. She felt bodies pressing in behind her, so close against her that she could not turn around to see who was pushing or if there was a way out.

Finally, she found herself in a large, open room. The first thing Mairead noticed were *sithichean*, the faeries. They appeared and disappeared, tumbled and twirled, shimmered and danced. They were everywhere, filling the room with motion of green and brown. And they were whispering, a constant buzzing and hissing that annoyed like bees.

The second thing Mairead noticed was the throne of moss-covered stone. Upon it sat a faery as beautiful as she was frightening. Her gown was made of silvery cobwebs, and a crown of leaves was woven through her long red hair. Her lips smiled, but her emerald eyes did not.

The third and most frightening thing Mairead noticed was the old, shriveled hag standing next to the Faery Queen. She was crooked with a hunchback and wore a dark green cape and hood that hid only part of her ancient, wrinkled face. In the arms of the hag lay Mairead's beloved son, Aonghas Beag.

The Faery Queen spoke. "What brings you here, mortal woman?"

"I am Mairead, and I have come for Aonghas Beag."

"And why should we give him to you?"

"Because he is my son, and I am his mother."

Immediately the room was hushed and still. The faeries, who have no mothers, did not move or speak, for they wanted to hear what a mother would do. Mairead and the Faery Queen faced each other across the room, and the only sound was a dripping of water from the roots and vines overhead.

"We hear," said the Faery Queen, "that you are good at baking. We will not give you Aonghas Beag until you give us the lightness of your hands."

The lightness of her hands? No more scones and biscuits for Aonghas Mor? How he loved her baking! But that was a small enough price to pay for the return of their son.

"Very well," said Mairead. "Take the lightness of my hands," and she extended them both toward the Faery Queen. The Faery Queen did not stand, but reached out, and although they never touched, Mairead felt the long icicle fingers stroke her hands. Then Mairead's hands fell to her sides, heavy as lead.

"Now give me back Aonghas Beag."

"We hear," said the Faery Queen, "that you are good at dancing. We will not give you Aonghas Beag until you give us the lightness of your feet."

The lightness of her feet? Mairead thought about how Aonghas Mor loved to dance with her about the cottage and how she loved to dance her son across the moors. Still, it was a small enough price to pay for the return of their son.

"Very well," said Mairead. "Take the lightness of my feet." The Faery Queen extended her two bare feet, and Mairead's own feet became as stone.

"Now give me back Aonghas Beag."

"We hear," said the Faery Queen, "that you are a happy woman. We will not give you back Aonghas Beag until you give us the lightness of your heart."

The lightness of her heart? Mairead remembered the many times she and Aonghas Mor had laughed together, and how full her heart was the day their son was born. She thought of the songs she and her husband sang, and the games they played. Yet how could there ever be song or laughter if Aonghas Beag was not with them?

"Very well," said Mairead. "You may also take the lightness of my heart."

This time the Faery Queen stepped down from her throne. She beckoned to Mairead, who stepped forward until the two stood so close that Mairead could see the flecks of gold in the Faery Queen's eyes, and a wilted brown leaf among the crown of green. The Faery Queen reached out with one hand and touched Mairead's chest, and immediately her heart was like marble, heavy and hard.

"Now give me back Aonghas Beag."

The Faery Queen laughed and turned away from Mairead, walking back to her throne. "Why should we? He is always happy with us here. He will never know cold or hunger, and he will never grow old here. Why should we let him back into your world of death and pain?"

Then Mairead knew the truth of the faery world. She knew they would never willingly give her back her son, nor let her return to the world above. With one leap forward she grabbed Aonghas Beag from the arms of the hag, and ran with him away from the Faery Queen. The faeries, with their unearthly screeching and screaming, rushed after her. Mairead could feel them all about her, their wings beating the air, and their hands grabbing at her son. Nearer and nearer they came, and with her feet and hands and heart so heavy, Mairead knew she could not run fast enough.

For just the briefest of moments, Mairead thought there was no hope. And then she remembered. "This will help you in desperate times. Keep it with you, always." The tired face and the clenched fist of the old man flashed through her mind.

Mairead reached into the pocket of her apron, and with the feel of the faeries' breath upon her neck and in her hair, she turned around to face the screeching horde, the rusty nail held high in one hand.

Whish! In no more time than it takes for a mortal heart to beat, the faeries were gone, for creatures of the Otherworld cannot bear the sight or touch or smell of iron or steel. Mairead regained the lightness of her hands and feet and heart. She stamped her foot three times—and there she was, on top of the knoll, with the brightness of the moon and stars above her. In one hand was the coldness of the nail, and in the other arm was the warmth of her wee *bairn*.

Mairead soon arrived at her home, where she found an empty cradle. She scrubbed it and filled it with clean bed linen. She bathed Aonghas Beag, fed him and laid him in the cradle and carefully hung the sprig of rowan on the cradle's hood.

Aonghas Mor returned the next morning from the market, coins jingling in his pockets. He listened to Mairead's story, and so happy were they to be all together again that the three of them danced the Reel of Tulloch through the heather and over the moors.

Songs

To a Wee Toddler

Maigean

This simple air is from Skye. "Maigean" means "dwarf" but refers to a little child who is learning to walk, and is pronounced "MAH-kin," "MY-kin," or "MAY-gun."

> They'll no get ye, Maigean,
> They'll no get my toddlin' wean,
> Toddlin' by his mammie,
> They'll no get ye, Maigean.
> They'll no get ye, Maigean,
> I'll no let ye to the well,
> Nor lift-in' o' potatoes,
> They'll no get ye, Maigean.

Uist Cradle Croon

Caidealan Cuide Rium Fhin Thu[1]

Like most lullabies, the sense of the words is not what is important, but the love and the security they express. This Lochmaddy air was collected by Kenneth Macleod from Mrs. Malloch, in Crianlarich. The words are from Isabel Macleod of Eigg.

> Sleepy one,
> Croon o' the wind and wavelet,
> Croon o' the wind and the waters,
> Sleepy one,
> Croon o' the wind and waters.

---

1. CATCH-el-an COOTCH-uh REE-oom heen ooo

Thou're my rowans,
Thou art my hazel nuts,
Sleepy one,
Croon o' the water,
My berries brown,
My cinnamon clusters,
Sleepy one,
Croon o' the water.
Sleep to the croon o' the wind in the branches,
The wave on the shore,
The whispering moorland,
Sleep to the croon o' the wind in the hazel,
The lap o' the waves by the whispering moor-land.
Chuilein a ruin,[2] ne'er wake till morning,
Sleep to the croon o' the waters.
My honey art thou on the tips o' the heather,
Sleepy one,
Croon o' the water,
My whispering sweet,
My bosom's desire thou,
Sleepy one,
Croon o' the water.
Sleep to the croon o' the wind in the branches,
The wave on the shore,
The whispering moorland,
Sleep to the croon o' the wind in the hazel,
The lap o' the wave by the whispering moor-land.
Chuilein a ruin, ne'er wake till morning,
Sleep to the croon o' the waters.

---

2. hool-IN ah roon; Child love, don't wake 'til morn

To a Wee Toddler

They'll no get ye, Mai - gean, They'll no get my todd - lin' wean

Todd-lin' by his mam - mie, They'll no get ye, Mai - gean. I'll no let ye to the well, Nor

lift - in' o' po - ta - toes, They'll no get ye, Mai - gean.

Uist Cradle Croon

Sleep - y one, Croon o' the wind and wave - let,

Croon o' the wind and the wa - - - ters, sleep - y one,

Croon o' the wind and wa - ters.

Thou'rt my

row - ans Thou art my ha - zel nuts Sleep - y one, Croon o' the

wa - - - ter, My ber - ries brown, my cin - na-mon

clus - ters, Sleep - y one, croon o' the wa - - ter

Sleep to the croon o' the wind in the bran - ches, The wave on the shore, The whis - per-ing moor - land. Sleep to the croon o' the wind in the ha - zel, The lap o' the waves by the whis - per-ing moor - land. Chuil - ein a ru - in ne'er wake till morn - ing Sleep to the croon o' the wa - - - ters.

©nancy chien-eriksen '01

The Baker and the Faeries

INTRODUCTION

Ronnie Boyd gave me the idea for this story, sitting in his kitchen surrounded by cups of coffee and old books about the history of Picts and Celts and Gaels and faeries. Ronnie is serious about faeries, and he has done much reading and thinking on the theory that they were, in fact, a race of small people, forced underground into the dunes, when other civilizations invaded the islands. He also believes that the Celts never lived on the Hebrides. "Many people won't like that I've said that because it would change history," he said, laughing.

"And there goes all that Celtic jewelry in the gift shops for tourists," I agreed.

"Aye, well, there you have it."

This is what I wrote about Ronnie in my journal:

He's a very energetic man, a chain smoker, and in constant pain from a broken disc after a fall on Eriskay. He's dedicated to Catholic missionary work in Ecuador and has just retired from his job of helping the elderly get grants for refurbishing their homes. He is generous and lively, and he gave me a delightful two hours of stories.

Neighbors came and went while I was visiting, and the telephone rang many times. It was obvious that Ronnie is a vital force on the island, and I found it wonderful that someone so involved with the practical matters of life is still interested in the mystical. He talked with much knowledge and enthusiasm of the second sense, the evil eye, and the faery folk. Ronnie chuckled as he told a "wee" tale of a baker who loves his own bragging and baking too much. I took his brief story, added my imagination and a bit of music, and created this story of "The Baker and the Faeries."

The Baker and the Faeries

Am Beicear agus na Sithichean[1]

Oatcakes, honey cakes, almond cakes, too.
I can bake anything better than you.
Shortbread, gingerbread, with treacle so sweet.
My scones are the best scones you ever will eat.

Am beicear a Bagh a' Chaisteal,[2] the baker of Castlebay, was at it again. Baking and bragging. Bragging and baking. While he measured the flour and kneaded the dough, he bragged. While he ground up the spices and beat the eggs, he bragged. While he sifted and grated and pinched and rolled, while he mixed and mashed and whisked and poured, he bragged. Before the sun rose until after it set, the baker of Castlebay sang his own praises, never seeming to grow tired of hearing his own voice.

But the village folk did. "*Bi samhach!*[3] BE QUIET!" they grumbled, as they paid for their bread or scones.

"Stop bragging," warned a friend, "or *na sithichean,*[4] the faeries, will hear you."

"And what if they do?" asked the baker. "It's the truth, isn't it? I am the best baker on this island."

"You're the only baker on this island," said his friend.

"Aye, that I am!" And the baker roared with laughter, for he loved a joke as well as the next man, even if it was about himself. "Maybe I'm the best baker in all of Scotland."

---

1. ahm BAY-ker AH-goos ahn SHEE-ack-an
2. ahm BAY-ker ah bahg ah KHASH-chul
3. bee SAH-vahkh
4. nah SHEE-uh-khun

"Maybe you are, and maybe you are not, but what I do know is that the faeries don't take kindly to someone bragging about something that the faeries do as well." The baker's friend lowered his voice to a whisper. "The faeries believe they're the best at everything, you know. And if they think a human disagrees, then they take the mortal into their world to prove it."

"Then prove it, I will!" exclaimed the baker.

"Hush, man. You don't know what you're saying. The faeries might not let you come back."

"Then I'll burn every scone I bake, until they can't stand the smell, or me, anymore!" And the baker laughed with delight at the image of faeries holding their noses and kicking him out of their den. Then he returned to his baking, all the while singing as loudly as he could:

> Oatcakes, honey cakes, almond cakes, too.
> I can bake anything better than you.
> Shortbread, gingerbread, with treacle so sweet.
> My scones are the best scones you ever will eat.

When the last scone was baked for the day, the baker closed his shop and walked home, whistling and singing all the way. His wife and three children greeted him at the door, eager for the gingerbread he had promised to bring for supper, and the baps for breakfast. He kissed them all, then told his wife what his friend had said about the jealousy of faeries. "What will you do," he laughed, "if the wee folk carry me away to bake for their supper and breakfast?"

She did not laugh. "Och, husband, do not tempt the magic. I could'na bear to lose you."

He kissed her again. "I promise you this, my love. You will not lose me. I will always come back to you, even if the faeries take me to the Otherworld."

The two of them went inside with their children, and shut the door. They did not see the tiny lights that danced around the house that night or hear the whispers that rustled through the grass.

In the morning, the baker kissed his wife and children good-bye and set off down the road toward Castlebay, singing his usual bragging tune.

> Oatcakes, honey cakes, almond cakes, too.
> I can bake anything . . .

Suddenly the baker stopped, for ahead of him, sitting on a rock at the side of the road, was a little girl, not much older than his own daughter at home. She was crying and not just a sniffle or two but great sobs and moans of despair, her hands covering her face.

"What's the matter, my dear?" asked the baker. "Did you fall?"

The girl parted her hands, and looked up at him with large green eyes. "Oh, the most terrible thing has happened. I forgot the cake."

"The cake? What cake?"

"The cake my mother baked for my sister's wedding. Oh, and it was a beautiful plum cake, with cinnamon and nutmeg and currants."

"And how did it happen that you forgot the cake?"

"My family and I came over yesterday in my grandfather's boat. The wedding is to be here on Barra, and I was told to take care of the cake. But in all the hurry, I forgot." The girl ended her talking, buried her face in her hands again, and wailed with grief.

"Well, now, that's not such a terrible thing," said the baker. "I'm *am beicear a Bagh a' Chaisteal*, the Baker of Castlebay, and we can just go to my shop and I'll bake another cake. I'm quite a wonderful baker, you know."

"Yes, I've heard about you," said the girl, peeking up from between her hands. "But I'm afraid there isn't enough time. Perhaps you could just come to my grandfather's house and bake something there?"

The baker was more than happy to help the poor girl, and he agreed. And for some strange reason it never occurred to him to ask who her grandfather was, here on the Isle of Barra. Instead, the baker just reached out, and the girl slipped her tiny hand into his.

WHISSHH! In no more time than it takes to crack an egg, the baker found himself underground, in what he knew was the world of the faery folk. All around him were the little people, some as beautiful as moonlight, others as ugly and twisted as the roots above the baker's head. They all seemed to be chattering among themselves, or laughing at the mortal who now stood in a room that could only be described as a baker's delight. Bags of flour and oats were scattered across the floor. Jars of spices covered the shelves. Piles of nuts dotted the tables, and everywhere were bowls of cream, tubs of honey, and crocks smeared with butter or treacle. No less than five paddles to lift out loaves of bread leaned close to the baking ovens.

"And what do you think of all this, Baker?" asked a voice that seemed to be the wind itself. "Do you think you could create 'the best scones you ever will eat' here, for us?"

The baker looked around the room to identify who had spoken. "And just who would I be baking for?"

"For the faeries, of course. And for their King." And there he was, *Righ nan Sithichean,*[5] the King of the Faeries, a tiny man, dressed all in green and brown, and standing no higher than the baker's knee. The only thing that set him apart from all the other faeries was a simple gold band that encircled his head. "We've heard, more times than we care to remember, that you are the best baker in Castlebay. Is that true?"

The baker laughed and quickly answered, "Aye, that's true."

"Then would you stay here a while and bake something for us? Perhaps a honey cake and a few of those famous scones?"

Now, the baker knew that faeries are not as willing to allow mortals to leave the Otherworld as they are to trick them into being there. He would have to be careful to make sure he could return to his family. "And how long would I be staying with you?" he asked.

The King pointed to a sack of flour close to the baker's foot. "Only until you have used all the flour in that wee bag."

"Och, that's not so bad. I promise you the best cakes and breads and scones you've ever tasted. And then, in no more than a week, I'll be leaving you and going home to my family. Is that agreed?"

"It is agreed that you will be going home as soon as all that flour is baked."

"Well, then, I'd better begin my work. I have a wife, three children, and an entire village who can't wait for me to return." The baker laughed, rolled up his sleeves, and began to do what he did best—baking.

And bragging. All the time that he was measuring and mixing, he was also singing.

Oatcakes, honey cakes, almond cakes, too.
I can bake anything better than you.
Shortbread, gingerbread, with treacle so sweet.
My scones are the best scones you ever will eat.

---

5. ree nun SHEE-ack-an

The baker was sorry to be away from his family for a week. But as he lifted his first honey cake off the paddle, he thought of *sgeulachdan*,[6] the stories he could tell his children when he returned from the Otherworld. While he mixed the flour and buttermilk for his scones he listened to *ceol*,[7] the music of fiddles and bagpipes and drums, and tried to remember the tunes so he could sing them to his friends above ground. Later, while the gingerbread baked, he danced a *ruidhle*,[8] a reel, with the faeries, memorizing the steps so he could teach them to his wife. Best of all, when anyone stopped by for a piece of shortbread or a bannock, the baker enjoyed each delighted smack and swallow that the faeries made as they devoured his creations. He could see that they liked his baking, and he believed that *Righ nan Sithichean* would honor the agreement and give him his freedom, in no more than a week.

But time in the Otherworld is not the same as time in the Mortal World, and a faery's agreement is often made with *sannt*,[9] greed, and *draoidheachd*,[10] magic.

It might have been an hour, or perhaps a day, or maybe even a week, that had passed by when the baker thought to himself, "How very odd. My fingers are cramped from all the kneading, my back is weary from the many hours I've been on my feet, and my voice is so tired from singing that I can sing no more today. Yet the bag of flour appears as full as when I began. I must have been doing more dancing than I thought. I will have to work harder if I am ever to be home with those I love."

He baked and he baked and he baked. With no idea whether it was day or night, the baker made the baps his family loved for breakfast and the almond cakes his customers loved for tea. All the while he was thinking. "This bag is never going to finish." He even considered dumping the flour behind a rock, but there were always faeries close by, either devouring his delicious goods or chattering among themselves and watching him closely. None of them seemed to care about how tired he was, nor did they listen to his pleas for an explanation about the flour.

Then, one day, there was a great deal of commotion and confusion as the faeries all gathered around their King, and WHISSHH! In no more time than it takes to pinch salt, the faeries were gone, leaving behind only one old faery, shriveled with time. He sat close to a peat fire, smoking a pipe and staring at the baker.

---

6. SKEE-lahk-un
7. kyohl
8. RYEE-uh-luh
9. sount
10. DROO-ee-ahkh

"Where did they go?" asked the baker.

"Above."

"Why?"

"To see what there is to see."

"Oh, why could they not take me with them?" And the poor baker, tired and lonely and sick at heart for the sight of his own hearth and home, began to weep. The tears rolled down his cheeks and splashed onto the flour-covered table. He never stopped his work, but continued baking and crying, crying and baking.

For a long while the old faery sat in silence, fascinated by the baker and his tears, for faeries cannot truly cry. When the baker's sorrow had diminished to only an occasional sniffle, the faery looked away, puffed on his pipe, asked, "Would you like to know why it is that the bag never empties?"

The baker stopped and stared. "Aye, that I would," he barely breathed, afraid to move and startle the faery from revealing the secret.

"The King won't like it if I tell you," said the old faery, "but I've grown weary of listening to your singing."

The baker said nothing.

"And your scones are not the best. I've tasted many that were better."

The baker nearly choked, but still said nothing.

"But your gingerbread. . . . Och, well, I will miss your gingerbread."

The baker managed a thin smile.

"Well, here's the answer. Every time you finish baking there's always flour left over on the table. You gather that together, and you put it back into the bag. Now, if you would throw that flour away each time, the bag would empty. That's it, then."

For a moment, the baker remained silent. Then, knowing that a faery cannot directly tell a lie, the baker clapped his hands, shouted "*TAPADH LEIBH!*[11] THANK YOU!" and, with one sweep of his great arms, brushed all the flour off the table and onto the floor. Then he returned to his baking. With hope restored in his heart, he kneaded and mixed and shaped and iced—and sang.

"Oatcakes, honey cakes, almond cakes, too . . ."

"NO MORE SINGING!" shouted the old faery.

The baker laughed and laughed. "Right you are, then. No more singing."

---

11. TAH-puh lev

In no time at all, the baker noticed that the flour in the bag was going *sios, sios, sios*[12], down, down, down. When the faeries returned, a few hours—or was it days?—later, the bag was *falamh*,[13] empty.

Righ nan Sithichean was furious. "Did someone tell you how to empty the bag?" he hissed.

The baker ignored the question. "You told me I would get my freedom when the bag was finished. Now you must keep your word."

"I will keep my word," said the King. "But someone will pay dearly for telling my secret!" He looked long and hard at the old faery, still sitting by the fire with puffs of pipe smoke curling around his pointed ears. "Now prepare yourself, baker, for the world you left behind."

The baker rolled down his sleeves, brushed the flour off his hands, and picked up a golden platter covered with squares of his gingerbread. He turned to offer it to the old faery who had helped him.

"Thank you kindly," said the faery, "but I don't think I'll be having the chance to enjoy gingerbread anymore." The baker looked into the faery's sad eyes, and then, WHISSHH! In no more time than it takes to cut soft butter, the baker found himself back on the road, in the world of mortal folk.

Running as fast as his strong legs were able, he set off toward his home. But when he got to the place where he knew it would be, he did not find a familiar cottage with smoke curling out of the chimney, and wife and children welcoming him at the door. Instead, all he found were the stony ruins of someone's home from long ago, cold and silent. Refusing to believe what his head already knew, the baker searched for some sign of his life, but found only rubble. He wandered out onto the moors, and it was there that he found a single grave, marked with a stone that identified the final resting place of his wife.

Suddenly, the baker felt old and weary, all the way into his bones. He sat down next to the grave, and thought about all that he had once known and loved. He knew that if he went into the village of Castlebay, he would find nothing familiar or comfortable. It was a strange world now; it was not his world anymore.

So the baker lay down in the heather and, filled with the stories and songs that few mortals have ever known, he fell asleep . . . *gu brath*,[14] for the rest of time.

---

12. SHEE-us, SHEE-us, SHEE-us
13. FAH-lav
14. goo brah

Faery Bread

INTRODUCTION

I found the idea for this story tucked into a fascinating and romantic book published in 1933, *The Haunted Isles, or, Life in the Hebrides*, by Alasdair Alpin Macgregor. True to the way most stories are given life, Macgregor explained that he heard the story from a minister, who heard it from two lobster-fishermen, who heard it from a man who lived on the Isle of Muck, who heard it from his two sons. And that is exactly how stories pass on and on, beginning with a bit of the truth, then growing with each telling, until it is difficult for the listener to find "the truth of it." So I created Rory to pass the story on again, and I can see him clearly and truly in the Otherworld of my imagination. Can you?

I believe that all stories are true, or at least possible. They just might not have happened—yet.

Faery Bread

Aran nan Sithichean[1]

Sandy MacDonald had two boys. The one called John was ten when he ate the faery bread, but it was Rory who ate the faery bread when he was seven and never was quite the same. People on the Isle of Muck wondered if he was a wee bit strange because of something he remembered or something he regretted. This is his story, exactly as he told it, over and over, to anyone who would listen.

"I saw a faery once. No, that's not the truth of it. I saw three faeries, and they were dressed all in green. I saw them standing on their faery boat, and I could have—I could have—ach, but I did not. So here I am, sitting before you, and you with that look in your eye. I've seen that look many a time before, and it won't scare me away from telling all the truth of what I saw that Friday morning. . . .

"My brother, John, and I were searching the beach for driftwood and treasures lost from ships and tossed onto the shores. That's how I got that chair you're sitting on; it was washed up on the beach. And who do you suppose is wondering, each and every day, 'Now, when am I going to be able to sit down, what with my chair at the bottom of the ocean?' Hah!"

And then Rory would slap his leg and laugh until the tears rolled along the wrinkles of his face. If the listener didn't laugh along with him there would be a long silence, while Rory puffed on his pipe, and the listener wondered if the story of the faery bread would ever be told.

---

1. AIR-ahn nun SHEE-uh-khun

"It was Friday, and my brother, John, and I were searching the beach for driftwood and lost treasures and the like. We came to the cove, the one where the land points toward Ardnamurchan—do you know where that is? You do? Ach, well, you're a smart one. I'll go on then.

"We found a tin that had never been opened. Of course, we wanted to know what was inside. Paint, perhaps. Biscuits, most likely, and we were hungry. So we banged it on rocks, pulled at it with our fingers, and knocked it about, but nothing worked and the tin stayed shut. Then John noticed a big stone, just lying in a crevice above us. So up we went, and we struck the tin with that rock, and that's when they appeared."

Rory took great delight in keeping his silence at that point. He would wait, as long as it took, for the listener to finally beg for more with, "That's when who appeared?" And off Rory would go again, his pleasure obvious as he leaned forward and held out his two big hands so that one was palm up, the other palm down, and no more than twelve inches from each other.

"Two little boys, no bigger than this. And they were dressed all in green, from head to toe. They just appeared, like stars that weren't there, and then they are. 'What are you doin'?' they asked, and John told them we wanted to open the tin. I said nothin' at all; I was too busy looking at their green vests and their green hats and the tiny green boots upon their feet. I remember thinking, 'I believe these are faery folk,' but I said nothin' at all.

"Then the wee boys asked us about our home, what our names were, and how often we came to that cove. Sometimes they spoke in the Gaelic, and sometimes in English, and I remember that I could understand every word they said to me. I know we asked them questions, too, but I don't remember any of their answers. Sometimes I'll hear a sound in the wind, or a word spoken by a child, and I'll think I'm going to remember—but I never do. I wish I could remember."

And then there would be silence again, an awkward silence, while Rory looked away and wiped his eyes, and the listener pretended not to notice. Then, abruptly, Rory would continue.

"What I do remember is the tiny boat lying alongside the cove. No bigger than a baby's cradle, it was, but a complete boat with a beautiful cabin aft. And in the doorway of that cabin stood a little woman, and I knew right away she was the mother of the two boys all dressed in green. Standing beside her was a dog, about the size of a rat, and his shoulders were at her waist. It barked and barked, until she reached out and, very gently, touched it on the head, and then it was quiet.

"John and I walked down to the shore, to be closer to the boat. I felt so huge and clumsy, and me only seven years old. The two little green boys climbed aboard, and while John spoke with the woman—he doesn't remember anything they talked about; I've asked him many times—I just kept looking and looking at the boat. Everything was perfect, the sail, the ropes, the wee anchor, and a tiny fishing net that was no bigger than my hand is today. Best of all were the pots and pans, the size of my fingernails, hanging in the cabin.

"I tell you, it was the neatest, prettiest boat I've ever seen. And it was real, I tell you, not a toy, and not a dream. I don't care what the others have told you, I'm telling you the truth of it."

Rory would be angry then, and he would puff and puff and puff on his pipe, as if he could puff out his story and make it appear in the smoke that circled around his grey and silver head. He would walk about for a bit, muttering to himself, his hands waving as they drew pictures in the air. Then, suddenly, he would see his listener, and he would abruptly stand still as stone for a moment, as if surprised to find company. Then he would return to finish his story, excitement in his voice.

"The little woman asked us to come into the cabin and have tea with her and her sons. For some reason, her invitation did not seem odd to me, even though there was no way we could fit inside that wee boat. But John said, 'NO!,' and grabbed my hand and pulled me away.

"'Very well,' she said, in that lovely, soft voice of hers. 'Will you share our bread with us, before you go home?' She came out of the cabin carrying several loaves of bread, each about the size of a walnut. John agreed to that, and we ate them and enjoyed them, for we were very hungry by now. The bread was delicious, and with only two bites, our stomachs were full.

"Then the little green boys said, and I remember these words quite clearly after eating the faery bread, 'When you see our boat out at the *Sgeir Dubh*[2] (and they pointed to a certain black rock not far from the shore), 'then you must return home. We will not be coming back here anymore, but others of our kind will be coming.'

"The next thing I remember was my sister's face peering into my own, and her shouting, 'What are you doing here?' So we went home with her, and I trembled with cold all the way, even though it was a fine summer morning."

That would be the end of Rory MacDonald's story. At least, it would be the end for the listener who was eager to say his farewell, and quickly hurry away from the strangeness of Rory's memories. But for those who stayed a bit longer, they would be rewarded by the chance to see Rory shuffle across the room, open a cupboard, and pull out a tin box, heavily dented and scratched. Then he would shuffle back, place the tin box in the listener's hands, and say:

"It's never been opened, you know. I've gone back to that crevice, but the stone is gone. I've tried other rocks, and tools and hands, but nothing will open it. What do you suppose is inside?"

Then he would wait, while the listener turned the tin around and shook it and tried to pry off the lid.

"Do you want the truth of it? So do I, child, so do I. Because you see, he told me, 'Others of our race will be coming.' And that is why I must keep the story alive."

Sandy MacDonald had two sons. The one called John is dead and gone. But Rory, my father, is the one who taught me to wait and listen, so I could find the truth in the story. And I believe I have.

---

2. skare doo

Songs

The Land of the Little People (Dream-Sail-Hoisting)

Air Eilean Mhara Nach Traigh[1]

The tune and the Gaelic come from North Bay, Barra, but the English verses are from Robert Louis Stevenson's "The Little Land."

When at home alone I sit,
Hee o vee hiu[2] o
And am very tired of it,
Hee o vee hiu o
O horyin o
Hoo-a-ho-ro
Hee o vee hiu o.
I have just to shut my eyes
Hee o vee hiu o
To go sailing thro' the skies,
Hee o vee hiu o
O horyin o
Hee o vee o
Hee o vee hiu o.
To the faery land afar,
Hee o vee hiu o.
Where the little people are,
Hee o vee hiu o
O horyin o
Hee a vee o
Hee o vee hiu o

Where the clover tops are trees,
Hee o vee hiu o
And the rain-pools are the seas,
Hee o vee hiu o
O horyin o
Hoo a ho ro
Hee o vee hiu o
O dear me that I might be
Hee o vee hiu o
Sailing on that rain-pool sea.

---

1. air AYE-len VAH-rah nock try
2. hew

The Land of the Little People
(Dream-Sail-Hoisting)

When at home a - lone I sit, Hee o vee hiu o.

And am ve - ry tired of it, Hee o vee hiu o. O

hor - yin o, Hoo - a - ho - ro, Hee o vee hiu o.

I have just to shut my eyes, Hee o vee hiu o.

To go sail - ing thro' the skies, Hee o vee hiu o. O

hor - yin o, Hee o vee o, Hee o vee hiu o.

To the fai - ry land a - far Hee o vee hiu o.

Niall of the Nine Hostages

INTRODUCTION

Who was Niall of the Nine Hostages?

- "Niall was High King (of Ireland), A.D. 379–405, and was the progenitor of the Ui Neill dynasty. He is recorded as raiding Britain and Gaul during the time of Theodosius the Great." (Ellis, 1992)

- "Niall is a shadowy figure. Some say he never existed, others that he did, still others that they can't be sure but think he may have, a reasonable conclusion in the light of what we know of fifth-century Ireland." (Roy, 1986)

- "The story of Niall of the Nine Hostages is an origin-myth in which the dynasty of the Ui Neill, descendants of Niall, was founded." (Green, 1996)

- "Niall Noigiallach, grandson of Muiredach Tirech, was High King of Tara, and his three sons, Conall, Eogan and Enday, completed the conquest of Ulster by setting up the kingdoms of the Northern Ui Neill in county Donegal." (Byrne, 1973, in which the date of Niall's ascent to High Kingship is given as "two generations" after the fall of Emain Macha, A.D. 327 or 331/332.)

🌀 "He ruled over the Ulster half of Ireland from A.D. 379 until his death in 405. His dynasty ruled Ireland until A.D. 1002." (Stone, 1998)

What is meant by "Of the Nine Hostages?"

🌀 "Niall's 'hostages' were the slaves and noble youths he brought back. For such extensive operations, nine hostages would seem a mere pittance; but perhaps they were very notable ones. Among them certainly was one Succet from Gaul, who was noble or even royal." (Nichols, 1990)

🌀 "The Airgialla, a confederation of nine *tuaths* [tribes], began submitting their pledges to the Ui Neill, from whence, it is claimed, derived the accolade." (Roy, 1986)

🌀 "The most plausible explanation of Niall's epithet is that it derives from the hostages received from the nine *tuatha* that originally made up the Airgiallan confederation." (Byrne, 1973)

🌀 "Scholars have concluded that to maintain the loyalty of powerful families, the High King would take hostages, normally youths, and keep them at Tara under something similar to house arrest. If the families did not meet their obligations to the King, those held might be ill treated or executed. . . . King Niall of the Nine Hostages, as his name indicates, has been cited as a prime example of this practice, and it is he who is credited with the interment of nine youths whose remains were found within the Mound (of Hostages, at Tara)." (Suits, 1995)

🌀 "Niall became known as 'Niall of the Nine Hostages' because of the captives that he took during his many raids of Roman Britain and the continent. Since he took hundreds of captives, these nine must have been of great importance, probably noblemen. One of the captives from western Britain was a lad of about sixteen named Succet. . . . The Irish and all the rest of the world eventually came to know him as St. Patrick." (Stone, 1998)

Trying to separate fact from fiction concerning the legend of Niall is much like determining what is true in the legends of King Arthur. But his significance as a High King of Ireland, his power as a raider and explorer of other countries, and his influence as the original ancestor of the clan MacNeil have kept his legend alive through time.

Niall of the Nine Hostages and King Arthur lived, and reigned, during the same era of British history, an era laden with wars and rich with stories. It is obvious that the stories did not recognize the boundaries of land but traveled within the hearts of the people and lived wherever the seed of "Once, long ago . . ." was spoken to a listener.

The following tale uses spellings from *Dictionary of Celtic Mythology* by Peter Berresford Ellis. It will be recognized by some for its similarity to "Sir Gawain and the Loathly Damsel," a legend of one of King Arthur's Knights of the Round Table, but it is also an Irish legend, a druid legend, a goddess legend, and a Celtic legend. It is a story of "Once, long ago . . . ."

Niall of the Nine Hostages

Niall Noighiallach[1]

I am the creation of truth and legend. I am the story told by firelight, and I drift with the sparks to become part of the ashes of earth and the stars of dreams. I am neither forgotten nor remembered. If you wish to tell my tale, you must listen to the song of the ancient Celtic soul.

History has given me the title Niall of the Nine Hostages. I am the youngest son of Eochaidh Muiglh Mheadoin,[2] High King of Ireland. There are those who say my mother, Cairenn,[3] abandoned me at the well from which she drew water every day. Others tell me she died when I was born. Ashes of earth, stars of dreams . . . .

It is the name of Mongfhinn[4] you must remember, for it was she, my step-mother, who destined me to be a warlord, forever proving my right to the throne of Tara. If my mother did abandon me, it was for fear of Mongfhinn. But there are those who say it was Mongfhinn who left me, a naked and helpless baby, to die, and it was Torna Eices,[5] a wandering bard, who found me, fostered me, and returned me to my father. There was neither joy nor celebration. Mongfhinn hated the sight of me, and jealously guarded the power she held over my father. So she sent me and my four brothers to Sithchenn[6] the Smith.

Sithchenn was a druid, and more. He was a prophet who could see with his Third Eye and tell what the future was to be. And what did he do but send all five of us into the smithy and then set fire to it, so that the flames of death burned

---

1. NE-yul NUY-yee-uhl-ach
2. AH-chee mwee VEE-an
3. KAHR-uhn
4. MAWNG-inn
5. TORN-ah AY-kess
6. SHEE-chen

over our heads and surrounded us. But we did not die that day. I swear to you there was music amid the roar of the flames, an ancient song that guided each of us to rescue a part of the forge. Brion,[7] the eldest, left with the chariot. Fiachra[8] took a vat of wine, and Ailill[9] removed all the weapons. Fergus carried out a bundle of kindling containing a stick of yew. And I? I stumbled out with the anvil, tongs, bellows, hammers, and all the tools of the smith's trade upon my back. It was prophesied then that I would be the greatest High King of Ireland.

And now I shall tell you another tale. Perhaps it will be familiar to you, for others have told it in later years, replacing my name with those of other heroes and lords. But that is how stories are passed on: from ashes to stars.

The story begins when I was a young man, eager to prove my strength and wisdom over my brothers, whose older years still gave them the chance to rule Ulster upon our father's death. We all knew the prophecy of Sithchenn, and yet it was still my task to establish my right to sovereignty. And so at every opportunity I struggled to be more clever, more charming, more powerful than they could ever be.

My brothers and I were hunting. The day was hot, and we had all developed a thirst that could be satisfied only by the cool water of the earth, not by the wine we carried in our flasks. So we separated, searching for a spring or stream. We agreed to meet again beside a certain tree within a few hours to compare our findings. Much to our delight, when we reunited Fergus said he had, indeed, found a well and could guide us to it.

"But do not be too anxious," he continued, " for there is a task you must perform that will perhaps prove to be more horrible than even your desire to drink can overcome."

"And what could be so horrible?" I asked. "Must we kill each other?" And I laughed, for I could not imagine anything worse than that.

"Come and see," he replied, and so we followed him to the well.

I tell you now that my brother's words of warning were not an exaggeration of the truth. The task was horrible, and it is only because of the shadows of time that gentle our memories that I am able to tell you what I saw and did that hot evening.

Standing by the well was a hideous hag, and I do not mean by this that she was a withered, old woman. No, this creature was disfigured far worse than what the years of a hard life can do. She was shriveled and twisted, with a hunchback.

---

7. BREE-unh
8. FEE-ah-chra
9. AY-leel

One eye was only half open, and the other was milky and colorless. Spittle dripped from her slack mouth, and when she smiled at us I saw that what few teeth were left were black and broken. Her white hair hung in long, greasy strands, and her skin was covered with boils that oozed their fatal sickness. But it was the stench that was worst of all. Even today I can remember how it filled our nostrils, causing us to gag, and how it took every bit of my self-control to keep from retching. I could only imagine what caused the brown and crusted stains upon her ragged dress.

She laughed. As we covered our mouths and pinched our noses, she laughed at our horror, which became even worse as we watched her lift her dress to scratch and pick at the scabs and blisters. And then she spoke, in a voice that wheezed and rattled with the leprous death we knew was approaching quickly.

"What is it that you desire, my lords? The pleasure of my womanly gifts?" She laughed again, and then broke into a long spasm of coughing. When it stopped, she spat, and wiped the drool on the back of one hand, and spat again.

"We desire water," said Brion. "Is it—clean?"

"And what makes you think it would not be?" The answer seemed obvious, and none of us replied. She gave another hideous smile, delighting in our discomfort and revulsion. "You may be assured that the water, unlike what you so unwillingly see before you, is clean."

"Then may we drink?" asked Fiachra. "We have been hunting this hot day, and we long to satisfy our thirst."

"As do I," she replied. "As do I."

"Then why do you not drink from the well?" I asked.

The hag gazed at me, her half-open eye twitching and the other blindly staring. "Because that is not the thirst of which I speak." The hag took a step closer to me, and the smell almost brought me to my knees. "There is a price you must pay before you may drink from this well."

"Gladly we will pay!" Ailill held out a bag of coins and shook it enticingly.

"It is not your gold that will pay my price." She turned and walked back to the well. "This water is worth more than gold."

"Tell them," said Fergus, "what you require."

Slowly she turned, and she looked at each of us for a long and silent while. "The payment, my lords, is a kiss."

I remember that, at first, I believed her comment to be in jest, a dare that even she could not expect anyone to accept. I laughed, and slapped Brion on the back. "You're the eldest. It is your right to enjoy her first," and I pushed him forward.

Her head snapped around, and she glared at me with hatred. "I do not offer this to amuse you," she hissed. "Either you willingly kiss me, or you cannot drink from this well."

"That is ridiculous!" Brion strode forward. "I will drink, and I will give you nothing." When he reached the well he bent forward—and screamed in pain as a thousand bees swarmed around him, stinging his face and hands. Brion fell to the ground, and as he crawled away from the well, more and more of the bees flew away, until, by the time he returned and stood next to me, the insects were gone.

"Does anyone else wish to try?" asked the woman. "I promise you worse than bees." She waited, but none of us moved. Brion continued to moan in pain, his face so swollen that he was no longer recognizable as my brother.

"Only a kiss, my lords, and you may drink all that you want."

We stood in silence, occasionally glancing at each other and at this night-marish creature that was obviously more—or was it less?—than human. I wondered if she tortured us with this bargain because she truly had feelings of loneliness, or only because, like many of the Otherworld, she existed to create havoc and unhappiness for us mortals. Was it worth the brief torture of a kiss, or would there be everlasting penalties to pay? Would she keep her word? And what if we all refused? Would our lives be the payment then?

Finally, Ailill spoke. "Brothers, we can do this horrible thing. It is just a kiss, after all. I will go first, quickly, with my eyes closed. And then you each will follow. Agreed?" We agreed. But when Ailill stood before the hag, his eyes opened and he could not shut them. And because he could not avoid seeing or smelling her putrefying body, Ailill turned and ran away. Fergus tried next, but he retreated in equal haste. Even Brion failed, although he saw her ugliness through eyes that opened hardly at all. Fiachra managed a hurried kiss upon her cheek, and then fled, rubbing his lips until I thought they would bleed.

And then it was my turn.

Good listener, I do not believe that you can possibly imagine how difficult it was to decide what I should do. One by one, I had seen my older brothers prove to be lacking in the courage that it took to perform this repulsive task. None was able, or willing, to be that strong or that wise. I could accept this challenge to prove to them and myself that Sithchenn was correct in his prophecy, and I was, indeed, the most qualified to be High King.

On the other hand, how could a kiss prove anything? What did the desires of one lonely hag have to do with my right to rule? And why should I, son of the High King, have to acquiesce to a woman?

That is when it suddenly occurred to me that perhaps the evilness of Mongfhinn was creating this horrific choice. She had tried, and failed, before to make me die in weakness. I decided Mongfhinn would fail again.

With eyes wide open, I kissed the hag long and hard upon her mouth.

What happened next is perhaps a miracle, or a mystery, or just part of the ancient Celtic song of the soul. I cannot explain how it is that all that was awful about her disappeared, and that what was left was a woman more beautiful than any I have ever desired, before or since that hot summer night. I will not describe her to you, for she is a secret in my heart to be treasured and remembered and treasured again. But I will tell you her answer when I asked her name.

"Flaithius,"[10] she said, and I knew it to be a word that meant royalty. "And it is you, Niall, who shall be the greatest of all the High Kings. Your brother, Fiachra, will reign briefly at Tara for the brief kiss he gave. But you will reign over Ulster, and people will know you as their sovereign for many and many a year."

Then she brought me the cool, sweet water of the well. I gave it to each of my brothers to drink, and they gave me their promise of Kingship in return.

That night, as the fire turned to ashes and the stars brought us light to dream by, Flaithius and I gave each other the pleasures of our ancient Celtic souls. I never saw her again.

My life was as she, and Sithchenn, foretold. All that I did, well, those are stories created by the mists and winds of time. My death was given to me by one of my own Leinster chieftains. But there is another death you must remember.

On the Eve of Samhain,[11] Mongfhinn, daughter of Fidach of Munster, and wife of the High King Eochaidh Muigl Mheadoin, prepared a poison drink to give to me, her stepson. She accidentally drank it herself, and they say that her evil spirit stalks the countryside in search of other children's souls.

Ashes of earth, stars of dreams.

---

10. FLAH-hee-uhs
11. SOUW-in; End of Summer celebration on November 1

Songs

The Ballad of Macneill of Barra

Oran Macneill na Barraigh[1]

This ballad tells the story of one of the descendants of Niall of the Nine Hostages. During the time of King James VI, Ruari, the "stormy" chief of the Macneils, was captured by treachery. Marjory Kennedy-Fraser collected these words from John Macneill of Eriskay, Mrs. Maclean of Barra, and Ann Macneil of Barra, demonstrating that the stories, and the pride, are passed on, one generation to the next.

Ruari Chief of Barra
Plunder'd ships of "good" Queen Bess
O-i-o-u-o fal-u-o
Ha-i-o o-hu
Him, the Scots King
O-hi o-hu
Trapp'd, betray'd and craven slew,
O-i-o-u-o fal-u-o.
Merchant vessel,
O-hi o-hu
By his castle anchor'd lay
O-hi-o-hu-o-fal-u-o
Ha-i-o o-hi.
Him, they offer,
O-hi o-hu
Wine and feast and welcome true
O hi-o-u-o fal-u-o
Ha o-i-o-hu.
While they're feasting
O-hi o-hu
Lies the ship in Castle Bay,

O-hi-o-hu-o fal-u-o
Ha o-i-o-hu
Song and harping
O-hi o-hu.
Sudden clamour,
O-hi-o o-i-o-u-o fal-u-o
Ha i-o-o-hi.
Out! *Mo sgian dubh*[2]
O-hi o-hu.
Traitors vile and black are ye,
O-hi-o-u-o fal-u-o.
Clos'd the hatches,
O-hi o-hu,
Sails the ship out to the sea,
O-i-o-u-o fal-u-o.
Vain, Macneill of Kishmul's vassals.
Vain, your cries along the shore.
O-i-o-u-o fal-u-o.
Ruari'n Turstar
O-hi o-hu
May return to Barra shore no more.

---

1. ORE-an MACH-neel nah BARE-eye
2. mo SKEE-an doo; my black (or dark) knife

The Ballad of Macneill of Barra

Ru - a - ri Chief of Bar-ra plun - der'd
ships of good Queen Bess. o - i - o -
u - o fal - u - o ha - i - o
o - hu. Him, the Scots King o - hi
o - hu. Trapp'd, be - tray'd and cra - ven
slew, o - i - o - u - o fal - u - o.
Mer - chant ves - sel, o - hi o - hu,
By his cas - tle an - chor'd lay, o -
hi - o - hu - o fal - u - o ha -

Vain, your cries a - long the shore, o -
i - o - u - o fal - u - o. Rua - r'in
tur - star, o - hi o - hu. May return to Bar - ra shore
no more.

Oisean of the Finne

INTRODUCTION

T his epic tale is part of the famous Fenian cycle, traditionally thought to have been created orally in the third century A.D., which depicts the adventures of a band of great warriors. In Ireland, they are called the *Fianna*; in Scotland, the *Finne* or *Fhinn*. These were men who fought under a strict code of chivalry and had to perform superhuman feats to qualify as a member of the group. Perhaps the most famous of these stories is that of Diarmaid and Graidne, a tragic tale of jealousy and betrayal, similar to the stories of Tristan and Iseult, and Deirdre and Noais.

The story fascinated me from the first time I came across a simple sentence in Katharine Briggs's *Encyclopedia of Fairies*: "Occasionally mortal men were invited to Tir nan Og, as Ossian was" (p. 400). I wondered why he was invited, not lured or enticed, and so I began to read about Ossian and Niamh and Fionn and all the other larger-than-life heroes and heroines of the Finne.

But it wasn't until I read "The Lay of Diarmaid" and "The Yellow Muilearteach" in *Popular Tales of the West Highlands* by J. F. Campbell that I began to understand why Ossian's story should be retold again. Donald Archie MacDonald (School of Scottish Studies) called Campbell's four-volume collection ". . . one of the great classics of oral tradition." Like Marjory Kennedy-Fraser and Kenneth Macleod's *Songs of the Hebrides*, Campbell's retellings are valuable not only for their authenticity but for all the scholarly extras included, such as the original Gaelic, the names and locations of the tellers from whom he collected the stories, and notes about other versions and the history of the stories. I have used Campbell's spellings of the names in my retelling, although there are other spellings that are more standard.

Among Campbell's copious notes for "The Lay of Diarmaid" I found the following comments about the Scottish origins of what is usually considered to be an Irish legend:

> *It is quite certain, then, that this old song has been preserved more or less perfectly by oral tradition in Scotland amongst people who can neither read nor write, for at least 330 years, and it gives a standard by which to form an opinion of popular traditions as an aid to written history.* (p. 261)

Campbell goes on to quote the collector of the piece, Hector Maclean:

> *This Laoidh Dhiarmaid is one of the most popular of the Ossianic pieces recited in the Long Island, and is known to more individuals than any other. In South Uist I heard it recited by Angus M'Donald, Janet Currie, Allan M'Phie, and some others; in Barra by Alexander M'Donald, and Donald M'Phie (smith), Breubhaig; also by a man in Minglay. The best reciter of this and other Ossianic pieces, that I have met with, is Donald M'Phie. This M'Phie says he learnt the poem from Neill M'Innes, Cill Bharraidh, who died about twenty years ago, about sixty years of age. M'Innes could neither read nor write.* (p. 261)

For me, that was the connection I needed, for here was proof that this tale has touched the hearts of storytellers and their listeners from one Celtic land to another. It traveled back and forth across the seas, from Ireland to the Hebrides Islands, later becoming part of the Highland Ossianic legends, popularized by James Macpherson's poem "Ossian." As Campbell says, "Let this tale . . . be taken as one phase of a myth which pervades half the world, and which is still extant in the Highlands of Scotland, and in Ireland, amongst all classes of the Gaelic population" (p. 285).

It is everyone's story, and it lives wherever there are those who want to hear about the days of long ago when there was magic in the mountains and the warriors were giants among men.

Oisean of the Finne

Oisean na Fheinne[1]

His name was Oisean, and he was a giant among men.

His name was Oisean, and he was a poet and a singer, and he told of the Finne, all of them giants among men.

His name was Oisean, and he had faery blood in his heart, for his mother was Sadbh, bewitched by the Dark Druid into the form of a deer because she had refused his love.

His name was Oisean, and he had mortal blood in his heart for his father was Fionn MacChumail, the last and greatest leader of the Finne.

His name was Oisean, and his name meant, "little fawn," for he was found by the hounds of Fionn in a forest glen.

His name was Oisean, and he was father to Osgar, who was killed as they fought side by side at the Battle of Gabhra.

His name was Oisean, and he was loved by Niam of the Golden Hair, daughter of the King of *Tir nan Og*,[2] the Land of the Young.

His name was Oisean, and for 300 years he lived with the faery folk in *Tir nan Og*, never knowing pain or illness or old age.

His name was Oisean, and the bards said he could "overtake a deer at its greatest speed and see a thistle thorn on the darkest night."

His name was Oisean, and he was a warrior whose legend lived on, long and long after the giants were gone.

The legend of Oisean began one summer day when the air was fragrant with sweet blossoms. A group of warriors gathered near the edge of a lake to rest and

---

1. AWE-shen nah heen
2. cheer na nawg

to remember their comrades who had been slain in the fatal battle of Gabhra. They talked of the gallantry of Osgar,[3] son of their leader's son, and how he died as a hero should, not meekly but in glory.

"You can be proud, Oisean," said one of the men. "He welcomed his fate, and his death was a triumph of honor."

Oisean said nothing. He stared at the waters of the lake, not remembering a great warrior, but a young boy with yellow hair and sad eyes like his mother's. Ah, his wife. How would he tell Eibhir of the Plaited Yellow Hair that her only son lay buried beneath the bloody earth of a battlefield? How would he find the words to sing the praises of Osgar, when all he wanted was to clasp Osgar's hand once more in his own?

Oisean had never lacked for words; he was a poet, and he sang the stories of the Finne more beautifully than anyone had before. He would recite their names and how they slew the great beast, Muilearteach.[4]

> *When they saw the wrath of the monster,*
> *Up rose Fionn[5] the Prince of the Finne;*
> *Up rose Oisean, Prince of the men,*
> *Up rose Osgar, and Iollainn.[6]*
> *Up rose Diarmaid o' Duibhne;[7]*
> *Up rose they, and Iall o' Buidhne;[8]*
> *Three sons of the dusky black King Dhuinne;[9]*
> *Up rose they, and Cearbhal.[10]*
> *Up rose Glaisean o' Damhach;[11]*
> *Up rose they, and Ard Amhard;[12]*
> *Up rose Ciar Dhubh,[13] Prince of Lomhann;*
> *The doughtiest four that were in the Fhinn,*
> *Went to do battle with the beast.*

---

3. OSK-ar
4. MUI-leer-toch
5. FEE-on
6. EE-yol-ain
7. JEE-arm-itch o DOO-yn-yeh
8. EE-al o BOO-yn-yeh
9. GOOyn-yeh
10. KARE-ah-vall
11. GLAY-shen oh DAH-ack
12. art AH-erd
13. KEE-ar goo

He had told the tragic tale of faithless Graidhne,[14] wife of Fionn, who betrayed him by loving Diarmaid, one of his own men, and caused his death because of Fionn's jealous heart. He sang of the great hounds, Bran and Skolawn, and of battles won and battles lost.

But now his own son Osgar, *Flath nam Fear*,[15] chief of men, was nothing more than a story and a memory. He was dead and would never again be fighting at his father's side, young and handsome and brave.

Oisean gazed across the flat, still waters of the lake and listened to the birds that called and sang, oblivious to his grief. The men of the Finne hunted, returning with a deer that had been relentlessly pursued by their hounds until their arrows found its heart. When the sun was high above them and the mist had been burned off the waters, the men lay themselves on the grass to rest.

Then, from the west, a rider appeared. At first the Finne noticed only the horse, a magnificent white steed that pranced its way on golden hooves toward them. And then they noticed the rider, a beautiful young woman with long, golden hair. Her eyes were blue, her skin as white as a swan's. A cloak, the same color as her eyes, billowed about her like marsh mist as she and her horse approached the warriors.

Fionn MacChumail, *flath na Finne*,[16] the chief of the Finne and father to Oisean, spoke. "What is your name, beautiful lady, and what is your country?"

"I am Niam of the Golden Hair, and my country is *Tir nan Og*, the Land of the Young. My father is the King, and we live far off in the Western Sea."

She was a faery, and Fionn, having loved a faery long ago, was cautious. "What brings you here among the Finne?"

"I have given my love to your son, Oisean. I have loved his strength since I first saw him lift a sword in battle. I have loved his words since I first heard him tell a tale. I have loved his beauty since I first saw him as a child, born to Sadbh in a forest glen. I have loved him, and only him, and have come to ask him to love me as well."

The faery's eyes rested on Oisean, and he returned her gaze. "Come with me, Oisean, and you will never again know the sorrow that fills your heart. Where I live, there is no death. Where I live, there is only joy and peace and love."

Oisean walked slowly to the faery woman, and wrapped his huge hands around hers that were no bigger than his palm. Fionn called to his son, but his son did not seem to hear.

---

14. GRY-neyh
15. flah nam fer
16. flah nah fin

"You are the shining one," said Oisean, "and it is you I choose. Take me away from this sadness."

"Oisean!" cried his father. "If you go, you will not return. I have lost my grandson; do not let me lose my son as well."

Oisean answered in a voice that was not his. "I am all over in love with her. I cannot stay."

"Come with me, Oisean," said Niam, "and you will have 100 swords and 100 robes of silk and satin. You will have more cows and hounds than you can count, and an army of warriors will await your call. Harpers will sing you to sleep each night, and my father will give you the diadem of the King of *Tir nan Og*. I will be your wife, and you will be forever young."

"I care nothing for robes or swords," replied Oisean. "I care only for you."

"Then I place you under *geasa*,[17] a word bond that cannot be broken. It allows you, a mortal, to enter the Land of the Young."

"Oisean!" cried Fionn one more time. "Will you leave your home, your wife, the Finne, forever?"

"I will leave death forever, father." Then Oisean kissed his father, but did not look into the eyes of Fionn, so he would not see the pain that was in his own heart. Then he lifted himself behind Niam, turned the white stallion away from the Finne, and rode back in the direction the faery had come.

Fionn whispered, "I have lost my son and will never see him again."

Oisean and Niam traveled until they reached the sea. When the horse's gold-shod hooves touched the water it plunged forward, galloping across the waves as if they were earth and stone. Far across the ocean the three continued, until the land that Oisean had once known was nothing but a shadow and then vanished into the light.

The horse never tired, but when they reached the shore of a rocky island it stopped. The great warrior saw a splendid palace glittering at the top of a cliff. "Are we in *Tir nan Og*?" asked Oisean.

"There is no beauty here that can compare to the beauty of *Tir nan Og*," answered Niam. "This is the Land of Virtues, and its King is the giant, Fomor of the Blows. His Queen is the daughter of the King of the Land of Life, and a sister of my tribe, brought here against her will. She has put him under *geasa*, which does not allow him to ask her to marry him until she can find a champion to fight him in single combat. Will you be that champion, Oisean, and save her?"

---

17. GEES-ah; a spell or charm

"I am one of the Finne, the greatest fighting force of all time, and my father, Fionn MacChumail, was their greatest leader. Do you know how the Finne were chosen? No man was taken into the Finne until he knew the twelve books of poetry. And before any man was taken into the Finne he would be put into a deep hole in the ground up to his middle, with only a shield and a hazel rod in his hand. Nine men would cast their spears at him, and if he got a wound he was not thought fit to join the Finne. After that, he was to run through the woods of our homeland, with the Finne following after him to try and wound him. If he was wounded, or if his spears trembled in his hand, or if a branch of a tree undid the plaiting of his hair, or if he cracked a dry stick under his foot, he was not thought fit to join the Finne. And they would not take him among them until he leaped over a stick the height of himself, and stooped under one the height of his knee, and took a thorn out from his foot with his nail, all the while running his fastest. I can do all of this and more because I am Finne. I will kill Fomor of the Blows."

So while Niam waited by the shore, Oisean met the king of the giants. Fomor was a misshapen monster, a mixture of human and demon, with teeth and claws and a nakedness that reeked of rotten flesh. For three days and nights Oisean fought without food or rest, until finally Oisean remembered his father's deeds and his son's death in battle. His fury drove the sword up into the belly of the giant, and it shrieked its final curse, then fell to the ground and melted into the rocks.

The two faery princesses tended to the wounds of Oisean with healing herbs and gentle hands. The next morning he joined Niam on the horse, and they continued their journey to *Tir nan Og*.

"What will become of the daughter of the King of the Land of Life?" asked Oisean.

"She is part of an old tale," Niam explained. "Her part is played." Oisean never knew how the faery woman had come to be captured by the Fomor, or what her name was, or where she went after her freedom was won by Oisean of the Finne.

The white steed continued to travel across the clear, green sea, carrying the faery maiden and the mortal warrior. They passed many islands and cities and palaces. They saw storm-tossed waves around them, and wondrous creatures beneath them. But they were never harmed and the horse never tired, until finally they arrived on the shores of a country more beautiful than words could describe. Blue mountains, silver waterfalls, green fields full of flowers, and a palace covered with gems and gold were what Oisean saw, and it was so perfect that he could not speak or breathe.

"This is my home, and your home now," said Niam. "You will want for nothing, and all that I have promised, you will find and more."

From out of the palace came the King, who kissed his daughter and then clasped the hand of Oisean. "Welcome Oisean, son of Fionn. Welcome Oisean, who is to be the husband of Niam of the Golden Hair. *Ceud mile failte.*[18] A hundred thousand welcomes."

Oisean bowed and followed the King of *Tir nan Og* and his daughter into the palace. The feasting and celebration lasted for ten days, and on the tenth night he and Niam were married.

And so began years of perfection and bliss for the warrior who had once lived as a giant among mortals. Oisean loved Niam and gave her his whole heart. Their home was a splendid place of every comfort, and they never quarreled or sorrowed. Three children were born to them; Oisean named the two sons Fionn and Osgar, and his daughter was simply "The Flower." As Niam had promised, they wanted for nothing, and time passed so quickly and peacefully that Oisean believed he had been apart from his friends for no more than a few years.

But Oisean had human blood in his heart. The endless procession of days and years without conflict made him restless for the challenges he once had welcomed. He longed for a test of his strength, and he remembered with fondness the feeling of pride when his sword had slain an enemy. Now a thousand warriors fought his battles for him, and he envied them.

Oisean began to spend mornings and evenings gazing eastward across the seas. He talked to Niam about his father and sang the songs of his homeland. He recited the names of the great warriors and told the tales of their great deeds over and over to his children. Finally, his longing to see his home again was more than he could bear and he asked Niam for permission to leave *Tir nan Og*. "I will return," he promised. "I only want to see Fionn MacChumail, *flath na Finne*, again, and clasp the hand of my father, as I have clasped the hand of your father."

"Oh, my love," sighed Niam. "I will not refuse your request, though my heart is heavy with a sorrow I have never known before. But I must tell you, husband, that your home is not as it was when you left. Your father and all his Finne are gone. Instead, you will find that the people are led by priests, and they speak of saints, not warriors."

Oisean would not believe his faery wife, and convinced himself that her words were created by the fear she felt at his leaving.

"I warn you again, Oisean, my beloved husband. You are looking for a dream, a memory that no longer exists. But I will give my consent, for I love you beyond keeping you. Only remember this: If you ever want to return to me, do not place your feet on the earth."

---

18. keed MEE-luh FAHL-chuh

"Of course I want to return to you," said Oisean. "And so I will do as you say."

"A third time I warn you, heart of my heart. Your quest will not bring you the peace you long for. And remember: If you ever want to return to me, do not place your feet on the earth."

Oisean promised. The same white steed was brought to him that he and Niam had ridden when they first left the mortal world. As he rode back across the sea, leaving the Land of the Ever Young behind, all he could see was the grief upon the face of his faery wife.

Nothing was the same. Just as Niam had warned him, his homeland was gone. Even the shoreline was changed, for now there were fishing huts where once there were forts. Only crumbling walls were left of the castles he had once entered, and there was no sign of Fionn and his men. Roads led in all directions. Strangest of all was the size of the human folk, for they all seemed to have dwindled in height and strength. Horses were smaller, too, and Oisean rode among the people and their steeds like a giant among men. When he tried to speak, the mortals stared at him, in awe of his beauty and majesty. What they saw was a man at least twice the size of a normal man, riding a pure white horse with hooves of gold. The giant's hair was the color of the sun, his eyes were a piercing blue, and his robes were the colors of every flower in the fields.

When he asked about Fionn, only one replied, "Fionn? You mean the hero of legends? I have heard those stories about him and his Finne, but they lived long ago and are no more."

"How long ago?" asked Oisean.

"Three hundred years or more. And who are you to ask these questions as if these warriors were friends of yours?"

"They were friends of mine, for I am Oisean, son of Fionn. I am Oisean, poet and singer of stories. I am Oisean, the last warrior of the Finne."

"I have heard of Oisean. They say he went with a faery woman to *Tir nan Og*. The stories say that his father and his friends searched for him until their death, but he was never seen again."

"And so I, too, am but a story and a memory," thought Oisean.

Just then Oisean heard the shouts and groans of many men. He followed the sounds and came upon a crowd of people in a glen. Three of them were vainly trying to lift a great stone, but when they saw Oisean they scattered, pointing at the great warrior and chattering about his magnificence. Oisean was amused, but he greeted them courteously and offered to give them help, for his hand upon his thigh was as big as two of theirs. He could see that men had shrunk while he had been in the Land of the Ever Young, and because they were weak and he was strong he leaned from the saddle to push away the rock.

The human folk later said they heard a great clap of thunder as the saddle girth strained and snapped. Oisean, a giant among men, fell to the earth.

When Oisean awoke he found himself staring at the sky. He could not sit up, for his bones ached and his knees would not bend. Oisean looked at his hands, and found that they were withered and twisted with old age. When two of the countryfolk leaned over him and asked, "Do you need help, Old Father?" he saw a white-haired, bearded, feeble old man reflected in their eyes.

Oisean was brought to Saint Patrick to be converted to Christianity, but the ancient warrior replied that he would not wish to spend eternity in a Heaven that did not welcome the Finne, or live with a God who did not consider Fionn as a friend.

"I am Oisean, son of Fionn, *flath na Finne*, chief of the Finne. I am the father of Osgar, *Flath nam Fear*, chief of men. I am the last of the Finne, and it is long the clouds are over me tonight."

He spent the last of his days singing his own sorrow. He sang of hunting with the hounds and of heroes who were greater than men. He sang of *Tir nan Og* and of a beautiful faery woman with long golden hair. He sang from the blood that ran through his heart, both faery and mortal, and of the two magical worlds he had lost, both faery and mortal. The blindness that came upon him was a comfort, for then he could see only his memories.

When he drew his last great breath and his heart was still, Niam's faery heart could beat no more and she faded and drifted away, like dandelion seeds on the wind.

His name was Oisean, and he was a warrior whose legend lived on, long and long after the giants were gone.

Songs

The Lay of Diarmaid

An Laoidh Diarmaid[1]

Kenneth Macleod's retelling of "The Lay of Diarmaid" is a jewel in *Songs of the Hebrides*. The rhythm and beauty of his words roll across the tongue like waves across the sea:

> *And och! och! sure, mischance was in Fate that day, for who was standing in the door but Grainne, wife of Fionn, loveliest of women, the choice-one of Alba and Erin and every country on which a tale is put. No sooner got she a glimpse of the Beauty-spot than she took for Diarmad the full-love of her heart, and deeper was that love than the deepness of the sea, and stronger than the sun of the thaw.* (Kennedy-Fraser and Macleod, p. 112)

The song comes from Janet Macleod on the Isle of Eigg. The words are sung by Grainne as she grieves over the death of her lover, Diarmaid. Grainne was wife to Fionn but betrayed him by loving one of his warriors. When Diarmaid is fatally gored by a wild boar, Fionn refuses to give him the water that could heal his wounds saying, " 'What is fated must happen.' . . . 'Diarmad it was, Dearg it is' " (Kennedy-Fraser and Macleod, p. 110). "And that night Grainne, Love-of-women, kept the death-watch over Dearg, and made the Lay to him which the sorrow-women of the wake still sing. And next morning, when they were putting him into the grave along with his hawk and hound, sudden-leapt Grainne in beside him—and she and Dearg were left in the Death-sleep side by side."

> Dearg, son of Dearg, I am wife of thine
> Thee would I cause neither pain nor sigh.
> Thee would I cause neither pain nor sigh
> To each brave cometh ordeal of fire
> Blacker my fate to be left behind.
> Dearg, son of Olla, of the guiding heart

---

1. ahn LOO-ee JEE-arm-itch

Thou who could'st skillfully play the harp.
Thou who could'st luringly play the harp
Blood-fury left on thee stain nor mark
Though low-laid by the boar at last.
Dearg son of Alla, who fight-joy'd the Fayne
Gone like the sun that put stars to shame.
Gone like the sun that put stars to shame.
Deaths three keen-pointed in life they blade
Though thou tonight now art deaf to fame.
I see thy hawk and I see thy hound
Keen in thy love their hunt-trail they found.
Keen in thy love their hunt-trail they found
Dear to thee were we all three I trow
Now let all three be to thee for shroud.
Shed we no tear on our brave, but sing
That we tonight death-watch a king.
That we tonight death-watch a king.
Stately calm, open handed our mien
For we tonight death-watch a King.

The Lay of Diarmaid

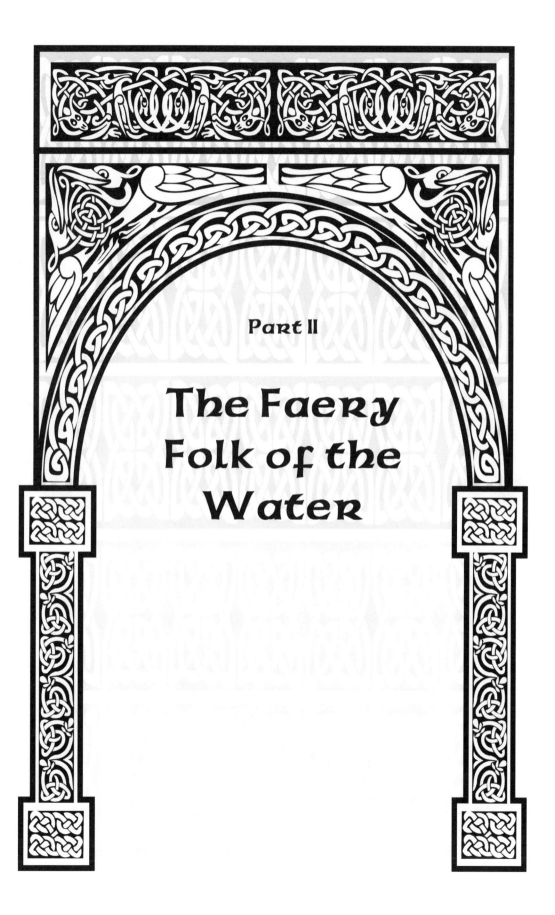

Part II

The Faery Folk of the Water

The Kelpie and the Girl

INTRODUCTION

I keep a file of stories that I will tell "someday," and this one was tucked into that file for more years than I can remember. I'm sure I saved it because it mentions Barra, but I never made the story mine because I knew nothing about kelpies. And so it was forgotten.

When I began doing research for this book, I went through those over-stuffed files and found "The Water Horse of Barra." I read everything I could find on kelpies, and I knew I wanted to tell this story of how love and patience tamed this most evil of the faery creatures. Now I see that it was meant for me all along, for it combines so many things that have been important to me in my life: horses, music, stories told by my grandparents, and the power of love. "The Kelpie and the Girl" has become a favorite of mine to tell.

In the misty Scottish isles, one can easily get lost in the moors. I imagine that these horrific tales of faery creatures who eat their victims were created to caution children against wandering too far or approaching the water too closely. Perhaps Black Annis of Wales, La Llorona of Mexico, and the Hairy Man of the southern United States are all waiting for us if we don't listen and obey those who tell us the stories.

The Kelpie and the Girl

An T-each-uisge agus an Nighean[1]

A kelpie lived at the bottom of a loch on the island of Barra. *"Each-uisge,"* the people whispered in terror, for that was its Gaelic name. *"Thoir an aire.*[2] Be careful," they warned one another, for they knew that the kelpie was the most feared of all the faery world. And why was that so? Because he haunted rivers and streams in the form of a magnificent black horse. Because his great brown eyes would hold a human as still as stone. Because this most powerful of all horses would move slowly toward his victim. And when innocent men or women or children were touched by the horse's warm breath, their fear would melt away. Eagerly they would place a foot in the silver stirrup that sometimes hung at the horse's side. They would settle comfortably into the saddle on the horse's great back and prepare for a quick ride home.

But home was never seen again. With a scream that was heard by no one except the rider, and with massive hooves crashing to the ground with no more sound than feathers in the wind, the kelpie would return to the loch. And as he began his descent under the waves, the man or woman or child would scream in terror. That scream was heard by those on the moors or those beside peat fires or those asleep in beds. *"Each-uisge,"* they would whisper, "Water horse," and then they would call out names to make sure that no family member or friend was facing a watery grave that night.

It was the bridle, some folks said, that gave the kelpie his power. "Take his bridle, and he must obey your wishes." Others said the only way of escape was to make the sign of the cross or call out to the Holy Trinity. But who could remember such wisdom when looking into the eyes of the devil himself?

---

1. ahn chekh OOSH-guh AH-goos ahn NEE-un
2. HOH-er un EHR-uh

For 300 years the kelpie lived on the Isle of Barra. He was feared. He was hated. He was lonely. The faeries that had taught him how to talk, how to take the shape of a man, and how to stand so still he seemed to be the night itself or move so fast he could catch a lightning bolt, were gone underground. There were no other kelpies. There was only the water and the wind and the darkness.

One fine spring day the kelpie was prancing beside the loch, tossing his head so that great silver beads of water fell all about him. Steam rose from his glossy skin, and he struck the pool three times with his tail, intending to return to the water. But just then he saw a girl sitting in the heather, watching over her father's cows. She was singing a spirited tune that made her laugh—until she saw the magnificent horse standing so near, and as still as death. He looked at her with great brown eyes, and she wondered many things. "How did he get so close without my noticing? Who does this horse belong to? And why is he staring at me so?"

Finally, the horse moved, gently lowering its head and stepping a bit closer. "What a splendid creature you are," said the girl, and, without even realizing she had moved as well, the girl stood up, reached out, and began to stroke the neck of the kelpie. To her dismay, she found she could not remove her hand.

"Och, no," said the girl, clever as well as pretty. "You are not a horse at all, are you?" And then she whispered the word she had heard in a story, told by her *seanamhair*,[3] her grandmother: *"Each-uisge."*

The kelpie spoke. "Aye, I am that creature you have known only in nightmares. And you are *ann am Barraigh*,[4] the prettiest girl on Barra. Therefore, I have decided to make you my wife." For in his loneliness, the kelpie had grown selfish and gave no thought to whether the girl could care for him as well.

Now, the girl knew she would have to keep her wits about her if she was to free herself from the magic of the water horse. So she answered carefully. "How very kind of you. But if I am to live with you in the water, I shall need a shawl to keep me warm. Will you sit with me while I finish knitting the one I had just begun?"

"That I will," said the kelpie. Immediately he changed himself into a handsome young man with hair the color of ebony and brown eyes that were cold and selfish from living alone for too many years. He sat in the heather with the girl, so close that he could smell the soap on her skin and see the golden lights in her long brown hair. And as she knitted, she sang, not the lively tunes he had heard earlier, but gentle lullabies, and sweet love songs that mingled with the scent of the heather and the soft buzzing of the bees.

---

3. SHEN-uh-ver; grandmother
4. OW-n ahm BARE-eye

When the kelpie yawned for the third time, the girl said, "Would you like to sleep a while?" He laid his head in her lap and was soon sound asleep.

"He is a very handsome fellow," thought the girl. "But I do not wish to spend the rest of my life married to a horse and living at the bottom of the loch." The girl tried to remember all that she had been told about how to escape from the power of the kelpie. And that was when she spied the silver necklace about his throat. "That must be the bridle," she thought. As gently as possible, she slipped the necklace over his head and then hung it around her own slender neck.

Immediately the kelpie woke and changed back into a water horse. But because he was in her power he could not speak, and could only look at her with eyes that were sad, yet still selfish.

"Now I shall show you where I live," said the girl. She led the water horse to her father's *croit*,[5] a small farm on the other side of the moor. "Father, I have brought you the finest and strongest horse you will ever see," said the daughter, and she placed a cow's halter around the kelpie's neck. "Never remove this halter, no matter how sad his eyes might be. And now I'm off to speak with the Wise Man who has *an da shealladh*,[6] the second sight."

The Wise Man listened to her story, but showed no sympathy for her fear of becoming the kelpie's wife. "Bring the water horse to me when you hear *a' chuthag*,[7] the cuckoo, sing over Barra. *Chi sinn na chi sinn*.[8] We shall see what we shall see." He took her gift of a bowl of crowdie, a cream cheese wrapped in a cloth, and shut the door.

Time passed. The girl and her father spent their days working the croft, with the kelpie's never-ending strength to help ease their burden. The giant horse did not tire, whether he was pulling a plow in the fields or carrying a burden to the market. He seemed to especially enjoy when the girl climbed on his back for early morning rides as the sun rose over the moors or evening rides as the sun set over the ocean.

Every night, when the work was finished and while supper bubbled over a fire, the girl would go to the horse's stable to feed him and groom him. As she brushed his long black mane she would talk of all they had done that day together and

---

5. krohch
6. ahn da HYAHL-uh
7. ah KHOO-uk
8. khee sheen nah khee sheen

thank him for making her life gentler. She told him about life on the island—*ceilidhean*[9] in the evenings, when friends and families would come together to share stories and songs, and the gatherings whenever a man and a woman were brought together in marriage, or when a child was born into the world, or when a loved one was to be buried in the earth. She talked of the seasons on Barra and how she loved them all, from the time of blooming heather to the time of angry storms across the sea. She would stroke his neck and scratch behind his ears and pet his warm muzzle, all the while singing the lullabies and love songs that had lulled him to sleep the day they met. Each night she would end their time together by blowing gently into his huge red nostrils so that their two breaths would become one.

Exactly a year and a day after she had removed the silver bridle, the girl was drawing water from the well one evening when she heard the cuckoo singing, and she knew the time had come. She fed and watered the kelpie, groomed him until his glossy black coat shone like the night itself, with sparkles of light in the darkness, and led him out of the stable. She mounted his back and rode him to the Wise Man, who was waiting for her, for he, too, had heard *a' chuthag* singing across the island that night.

"Take off the cow harness," he commanded, and she did. Immediately, the water horse took the form of the young man, taller and stronger than before because of all the hard work he had done at her father's croft. His hair was still the shiny black of a raven's wing, but his eyes—his eyes were altogether different.

"Now give him back the bridle," said the Wise Man.

"But then we'll be in his power," said the girl.

"Give him back his bridle, and *chi sinn na chi sinn*," said the Wise Man, who had looked into the kelpie's eyes. The girl took the silver necklace from around her neck and slipped it over the head of the faery man.

"Now," said the Wise Man to the kelpie, "tell us what you have learned during this year and a day."

For a long while the young man said nothing, only gazing into the eyes of the girl. When, finally, he spoke, it was with a voice filled with sadness and longing. "A year and a day ago I wished to carry off this girl and make her my wife. But I have learned that is impossible, for her life is here on the earth of Barra, and mine is beneath the waters of Barra's rivers and lakes."

The kelpie took a step closer to the girl, his eyes never leaving hers. "When the faeries left, and went underground, I should have gone, too. That is what I have learned."

---

9. KAY-lee-un

"Then you have learned much," said the Wise Man. "And if you had gone with the faeries, where would you be now?"

"On *Tir nan Og*,[10] the Land of the Ever Young, where there is no death or old age—and no sadness, such as I feel now."

"So you have known both—the powerful magic of being faery and the simple joy and pain of being human. If you could choose, which would you choose?"

The kelpie stepped closer again to the girl, and took her hands in his own. "If I chose *Tir nan Og*, I would live forever. But I would never again see these eyes or hear this voice or touch these hands. My breath would never again be one with yours. If I chose to be a mortal, I would not want to live without these eyes or this voice or these hands. Would you marry me, if I became a man?"

"Aye, that I would," answered the girl.

"Then that is what I would choose," said the man, who was no longer a kelpie just for having made the choice.

There was a gathering of family and friends for their wedding as had never been seen before on Barra and another celebration ten months later when their first child was born. It is true that the farmer grieved at the loss of the remarkable horse, but he rejoiced at the happiness of his daughter. And the brown-haired girl and her black-haired husband lived a long life together of great, and human, joy.

---

10. cheer na nawg

Songs

Land of Heart's Desire

Tir na Mhiann na Chridhe[1]

Tir nan Og,[2] the Land of the Ever Young, the Celtic heaven, is said to lie somewhere west of the Hebrides. It was believed that a great white barge would ferry the elect across the waves to the island where there was no pain or sorrow or death. It is where King Arthur rests and where the faery folk live in peace and pleasure.

Frances Tolmie collected this tune on North Uist, and Marjory Kennedy-Fraser gave it the English words about the Celtic paradise.

> Land o' Heart's Desire,
> Isle of Youth,
> Dear Western Isle,
> Gleaming in sunlight!
> Land o' Heart's Desire,
> Isle of Youth!
> Far the cloudless sky
> Stretches blue across the Isle,
> Green in the sunlight.
> Far the cloudless sky
> Stretches blue.
> There shall thou and I wander free,
> On sheen-white sands,
> Dreaming in starlight.
> Land o' Heart's Desire,
> Isle of Youth.

---

1. cheer nah VEE-awn nah KREE-yuh
2. cheer nah nawg

The Skye Water Kelpie's Lullaby

Cronan na Eich-mhara[1]

The words of this lullaby concern a kelpie who, in the form of a man, married a young woman and was the father of her child. But when the wife reasons that her husband's daily absences and the gravel around his neck identify him as the terrible water horse, she leaves him and her babe. Now the father sings to the child, in the hopes of convincing the mother to return.

Avore, my love! Avore, my joy!
To thy babe come
And troutlings you'll get out the loch,
A ho hi
A ho hi
A ho ho-an
A ho ho-an
A ho ho-an
A ho hi
A ho hi.
Avore, my heart! The night is dark, wet, and dreary.
Here's your bairnie neath the rock.
A ho hi
A ho hi
A ho ho-an
A ho ho-an
A ho ho-an
A ho hi
A ho hi.

Avore, my love! Avore, my joy!
Wanting fire here,
Wanting shelter,
Wanting comfort,
Our babe is crying by the loch.
A ho hi
A ho hi
A ho ho-an
A ho ho-an
A ho ho-an
A ho hi
A ho hi.
Avore, my bride! Avore, my heart!
My gray old mouth touching thy sweet lips, babe,
And me singing songs to thee by Ben Frochkie.[2]
A ho hi
A ho hi
A ho ho-an
A ho ho.

---

1. KROW-nahn nah ACHE-vara
2. Between Gesto and Portree in Skye

Land of Heart's Desire

Land o' Heart's De - sire, Isle of Youth, Dear West - ern
Isle, Glea - ming in sun - - - light! Land o' Heart's De -
sire, Isle of Youth!
Far the cloud - less sky stretch - es blue a-cross the
Isle, Green in the sun - - - - - - light
Far the cloud - less sky stretch - es blue.
There shall thou and I wand - er free,
On sheen - white sands, Dream - ing in star - - -
light. Land o' Heart's De - sire,
Isle of Youth.

The Skye Water Kelpie's Lullaby

A - vore, my love - - - A - vore, my joy!

To thy babe come and trout-lings you'll get out the loch,

A ho hi, A ho hi, A ho ho - an, A ho ho - an,

A ho ho-an, A ho hi, A ho hi. A - vore, my heart!

The night is dark, wet, and drea - ry.

Here's your bair-nie neath the rock. A ho hi, A ho hi,

A ho ho - an, A ho ho - an, A ho ho - an, A ho hi,

A ho hi. A - vore, my love! A - vore, my joy!

Want - ing fire here, want-ing shelt - er, want-ing com - fort, our babe is cry-ing by the

loch.   A ho hi,   A   ho hi,   A ho ho - an,   A ho ho - an,

A ho ho - an,   A   ho hi,   A   ho hi.   A - vore, my bride!   A -

vore,   my heart!   My gray old mouth touch-ing   thy sweet lips, babe, and

me sing-ing songs to thee by Ben Frockh-kie.   A   ho hi,   A   ho hi,

A ho   ho - an,   A ho   ho.

©nancy chien-eriksen 81

The Mermaid and the Selkie

INTRODUCTION

I often wandered the rocky beaches of Barra with two hopes. One was to see an otter, like the one in my favorite movie of all time, *Ring of Bright Water*. It is based on the true story of Gavin Maxwell, who lived in northern Scotland, befriending otters and writing about them in his books.

The second hope was to see a selkie, so I spent many hours singing to the seals that swam and lounged close to the shore. Their whiskered faces and curious, brown eyes make it obvious why, long ago, stories were told about selkies, who were seals in the ocean but could take on the shapes of humans when they came to land.

Unfortunately, neither hope was fulfilled. No one knew any stories of the selkies on Barra; perhaps they are better known farther north in the Orkneys. But the seals watched me as I watched them, and I knew my book must include them because the seals, and the sea, are so much a part of my memories of those sunny days on Barra.

One evening several months later, I was reading Katharine Briggs's *An Encyclopedia of Fairies*, and I found a "wee story," no more than a paragraph, about a selkie and a mermaid. "Ah," I sighed, "this one is for me." And that is how stories sing to our souls and are born in our hearts.

The Mermaid and the Selkie

A' Maighdeann-Mhara 'Us Fear-Ron[1]

Beneath the silver foam of the ocean, below the waves and beyond the pull of the tides, there lived, in a cave, a' mhaighdeann-mhara, a mermaid. It was not a cave of darkness, but a passage into light and all the colors of the sea. The mermaid, a creature of powerful beauty and grace, swam among the emerald sea grasses and lavender coral. She played with the crystal bubbles that rose from her mouth, and she allowed the rainbow-colored fish to hide in the tresses of her long, golden hair. And sometimes, when she could feel a sadness or a gladness within her, she would glide up onto a rock and sing of all these wonders with a voice that floated out of the cave and up into the world above, where the humans heard it and wept with joy.

The mermaid rarely came to the surface of the sea herself, for she had heard the tales of the mortal folk and how they captured the creatures of her world for show or money. When storms rose out of the sea, tossing ships and turning fishing boats over, she knew that either a mermaid or a selkie had died at the hands of a human. Then she would weep and sing and cry out the names of those she loved, to make sure it was not one of their deaths that caused the anger of the sea.

One of those she loved was a selkie. He was young and strong, sleek with the form of a seal and clever with stories of all he had seen and heard. He often went out of the sea and on to the shores to dance with the other selkies when they shed their skins under the full moon and became human in appearance. He would tell his friend the mermaid about nets and spears, and how he narrowly escaped them more than once. The mermaid would listen to him laugh about his adventures, and, although she envied him for his life of discovery, she often shuddered at the dangers she knew came with that life.

---

1. ahm MY-tchen-VAR-ah oos FER-rohn

It was a fisherman that was in Seumas. His father before him was *iasgair,*[2] a fisherman, and the father before that was *iasgair,* too. All they had ever known was a life of hauling in nets full of fish and mending nets full of holes. They cleaned fish, sold fish, ate fish, and followed fish out to sea. Seumas's grandfather died in his fishing boat when his heart could not bear the dragging in of the net, laden with glistening, silver fish, one more time. His father was lost in a sea storm, and Seumas's mother raised her son alone ever since he was of the age just between child and man. Now he lived with his wife, a young and fair lass who used to spend her time dancing with the men in town but now spent her days gazing out toward the ocean, wondering if Seumas would be coming home to her that evening. It was not an easy life, but it was enough.

Until she realized that she was carrying a child within her. Then, suddenly, their tiny cottage seemed too small. Soon after the birth of their son, the winds came from out of the north and Seumas's fishing boat was tossed onto the rocks and broken, as if it was no stronger than a seashell. He would need money to build another and to make his home big enough for three.

So it was that Seumas decided to sell the skin—of a seal.

The mermaid and the selkie played in the coral castles that grew out of the depths of the ocean. They dined on fish and rode along with the great whales, holding onto their barnacled backs. When they returned to the cave, the long white fingers of a full moon stretched across the waves, and the selkie was called away by others of his kind. It was a night to dance on the sand. The mermaid twined her hair about the flippers of her friend, and her blue eyes reminded him to be careful, to remember, to return. With a final flick of his tail, he was gone.

All that night, while the mermaid sang, the selkies danced. Their seal skins lay on the rocks, glistening in the moonlight. When the sun rose, the selkies dressed themselves in their skins again and returned to the water. But one stayed on land a moment longer than the others, and it was he that was clubbed by the fisherman Seumas, until he moved no more.

Seumas stared down at the seal, motionless at his feet. He knew the bloody task that lay ahead of him, and he wished that it could be done without his hand around the knife. As quickly as he could, he removed the skin, forcing himself to think of the food and lumber it would buy. When he was done, he walked into the sea to wash the blood from his hands and arms. Then he dragged the seal into the water and let the waves pull it away and down, from where it came. He returned to his friends who waited for him on the other side of the bay, and they set off in their fishing boat for the island of their homes.

---

2. EE-us-ger

The selkie tumbled down into the blue, and then the gray, and, finally, the black of the sea. But he was not dead. Cold, he was, and in a rage of pain and misery. Somehow, he had survived, but without his skin, it was only a matter of time before he would die.

It was the mermaid who found her friend, the selkie, lying on one of the rocks in her cave. His beautiful velvet skin was gone, and he stared at her with great brown eyes that told her all she needed to know of his suffering and fear. With the power of gentleness between true friends, she held him in her arms until he stopped shivering. Then she glided back into the water and began to swim quickly toward the surface, leaving a stream of silver bubbles, and her friend, behind her.

The mermaid knew that the only way to save the selkie was to find his skin and return it to him. As soon as her head rose out of the waves she saw the small boat that held three men, and, she was sure, the skin that belonged to her friend. Without considering the danger, she swam closer to the boat. She could hear the voices of the humans but did not understand the meaning of the words. It sounded harsh and cruel, like rocks crashing against each other. In her world, language was soft, like the lapping of waves on sand. The mortals seemed awkward, throwing their arms about as they talked and jerking their bodies, like fish cast out of the water.

It was, perhaps, these strange sights and sounds that caused the mermaid to be careless. The fishing net wrapped itself around her, and she could move neither her azure tail nor her webbed fingers.

"Seumas, give us a hand here. Something grand is caught in our net!" The two men pulled and heaved at the ropes, and Seumas left his daydreaming regrets about the seal's death to help his friends. But when the net was finally hauled out of the sea, it was Seumas who first saw just exactly what the "something grand" was.

"*A' mhaighdeann-mhara*" he whispered. "We've caught a mermaid. We must let her go, quickly, before she dies without the sea."

"Are you daft, man? Look at her. Have you ever seen anything so strange and beautiful?"

"No, I have not," said Seumas, staring down at her blue eyes that somehow reminded him of the brown eyes of the seal.

"Neither has anyone else on these islands. I just thought they were stories our grandmothers told us. But now we have something better than a story."

"What are you saying?" asked Seumas, kneeling to cup seawater in his hands and sprinkle it over the ivory skin of the mermaid.

"I'm saying that we'll keep this mermaid and show her to the people—for money. You'll have that boat before you know it, Seumas."

"I'll have the boat from the seal's skin I took earlier. I don't want to kill a mermaid, as well."

"Who said anything about killing her?"

"She can't live long without the ocean. Look at her. She's already fading."

It was true. As the three fishermen watched, the brilliant colors of the mermaid's tail began to lose their brightness. Her mouth opened and closed, but no sound was heard. Tiny fish flopped about in the tendrils of her hair, but she lay still, except for one hand that stroked the seal skin beneath her in the boat.

"We must hurry then," said one of the men. "Row, fast as you can, Seumas. We have a mermaid to sell!"

All the while that Seumas rowed back to the shore, he pleaded with his friends to return the faery creature to the ocean, but they would not listen. As strong as he was, he knew he could not throw the net with the mermaid out of the boat without the help of the other two men. He pulled and pulled at the oars, all the while watching the mermaid who lay quietly at his feet, her eyes closed now and her hand still clutching the seal skin.

As the life of the mermaid began to end, a storm grew in the belly of the sea. When the mermaid's last breath escaped in a tiny crystal bubble, a great wave swept over the boat, turning it over and sending all that it held into the watery depths of another world, forever. The body of the mermaid, the three fishermen, and the selkie's skin disappeared into the blue, and then the gray, and finally, the black of the ocean.

One month later, when the moon was again full and bright, the selkies came out of the sea to shed their skins and dance upon the shore. There was one among them who danced alone, all the while singing of the sadness within him. When the sun rose, and the selkies returned to the sea, he swam to a cave of lightness and color, where he gathered the faery creatures about him so they could hear the story of two friends and how one died so that the other could live and tell the story.

Songs

The Profound Sleep

An Cadal Trom[1]

In the first volume of *Songs of the Hebrides*, Marjory Kennedy-Fraser and Kenneth Macleod retell a story to preface this song. It explains that seals are the children of the King of Lochlann, *clann Righ Lochlainn fo gheasaibh*.[2] Their home was a mythological wonderland beyond the seas. They were put under spells by their stepmother, forcing them to be half-fish and half-beast because she hated their beauty, wisdom, and bravery. Three times a year, under a full moon, the seals return to their natural state, and their hearts are filled with sorrow and envy for the human life they cannot have. "And if you were to see one of them as they should be always, if right were kept, you would take the love of your heart for that one, and if weddings were in your thoughts, sure enough a wedding there would be" (p. 15).

This song comes from the grief of a seal-woman's heart, after a human carries her home in his arms but then releases her back to her own sea-kin when he realizes he loves a seal.

> Pillow'd on the sea-wrack brown am I
> On the gleaming white sheen sand, o hi
> Lull'd by sweet croon of waves I lie
> Could slumber deep part thee and me.
> Far away my own *gruagach*[3] lone
> On the gleaming white friend-reefs, o hi
> Lies, and that the cause of all my moan,
> Did slumber deep part thee and me.
> On the morrow shall I o'er the sound
> Oe'r the gleaming white sheen sand, o hi
> Swim until I reach my *gradh-an donn*,[4]
> Nor slumber deep part thee and me.

---

1. ahn CAT-al trum
2. clawn ree LOCK-lane foh YES-iv
3. GROO-ugh-ahkh; maiden
4. GRAH-yun doun; loved one brown

The Seal-Maiden

Gruagach-Mhara[1]

Early one morning,
Ho eel yo,
Stray sheep a seeking,
Ho eel yo,
Great wonder saw I,
Ho eel yo,
Fair seal-maiden,
Ho eel yo.
Glossy her dark hair,
Ho eel yo
Veiling her fair form,
Ho eel yo.
Heel yo heel yo rova ho,
Lone on sea-rock sat the maiden.
Heel yo heel yo rova ho,
Grey her long robe closely clinging.
Heel yo heel yo rovha ho.
When, great wonder!
Ho eel yo,

Suddenly changed she,
Ho eel yo.
Heel yo heel yo rova ho,
Raised her head she, stretched she outward.
Heel yo heel yo rova ho,
Diving seaward,
Ho eel yo.
Smooth seal-headed she,
Ho eel yo.
Out by the teal-tracks,
Ho eel yo.
Cleaving the sea-waves,
Ho eel yo.
Heel yo heel yo rova ho,
Through *Chaol Mhuile*,[2]
Through *Chaol Ile*.[3]
Heel yo heel yo rova ho,
To the far blue bounteous ocean!

---

1. GROO-ugh-ahkh–VAR-ah
2. kyle MOO-lah; Isle of Mull
3. kyle EES-lah; Isle of Isla

The Profound Sleep

Pil - low'd on the sea - wrack brown am I On the gleam - ing white sheen sand, o hi, Lull'd by sweet croon of waves I lie. Could slum - ber deep part thee and me. Far a - wa - ay my own gruag - ach lone On the gleam - ing white friend reefs, o hi, Lies, and that the cause of all my moan, Did slum - ber

deep   part   thee   and   me.

On   the   mor - row   shall   I   o'er   the   sound

On   the   gleam - ing   white sheen - sand,   O

hi   Swim   un - til   I   reach my

gra'dh - an   donn   Nor   slum - ber   deep

                                          part   thee   and   me.

The Seal-Maiden

Ear - ly one morn - ing, Ho eel yo, Stray sheep a

seek - ing, Ho eel yo, Great wond - er saw I,

Ho eel yo, Fair seal mai - den, Ho eel

yo. Gloss - y her dark hair, Ho eel yo,

Veil - ing her fair form, Ho eel yo. Heel yo heel

yo ro - va ho, Lone on sea - rock sat the mai - den. Heel yo heel

yo ro - va ho, Grey her long robe close - ly cling - ing. Heel yo heel

yo ro - va ho. When, great won - der! Ho eel yo,

Sudd - en - ly changed she, Ho eel yo. Heel yo heel

Legend of the Mermaid

INTRODUCTION

It is important for me to be able to believe in the possibility of the existence of the Otherworld, a world where faeries and mermaids and leprechauns, bogles and kelpies and banshees, live and perform their magic and mischief. I would like to believe it is possible that on an ordinary day, an ordinary person could have an extraordinary encounter with someone from the Otherworld. Most of all, I would hope that if such an encounter occurred, no evil would be done by either human or faery, but, instead, each would learn about the other, and then part, a bit wiser and gentler for the awakening.

That is why this story touched me so deeply when I discovered it in Norman Morrison's *Hebridean Lore and Romance*, published in 1936. Morrison was a naturalist, Gaelic folklorist, and a born *sgeulaiche*,[1] storyteller. According to D. J. Macleod, who wrote the foreword to the book, Morrison "grew up by the ceilidh[2] fireside, with a listening ear and an instinct to relate, in traditional style, whatever of interest he heard or saw."

---

1. SKEE-a-likh-uh
2. KAY-lee; gathering

Morrison knew that the stories of his people were disappearing. "In this age of competition and materialism, folk-lore and tradition are sneered at and stigmatised as a sickly sentiment and superstition of a bygone age of no value to modern civilisation" (preface). So he wrote the stories down, combining fact with romance, as "the best means of preventing them from passing into oblivion" (preface). The following legend is one he heard as a boy on the Isle of Lewis; as Morrison states, it "demonstrates the powerful imagination of the ancient Celt, and shows that he possessed the rare gift of garnishing and embellishing his myths in a most subtle fashion" (p. 99).

My retelling of this legend is a weaving of Morrison's story and what I hope is still possible in our own age of "competition and materialism." It is also a tribute to all the Celts before me who gave it their own breath of magic and mischief.

Legend of the Mermaid

Seanachas na Maighdinn-Mhara[1]

The storm had passed. *Eoghann na Mara*,[2] Hugh of the Sea, made his way along a remote part of the west coast of the Isle of Lewis. It was low tide, and Hugh was searching the beaches for driftwood or other materials left on shore.

Hugh was a giant of a man. He was in his middle years, content with a wife, a daughter, and a son. Like most of the men on the island, his calling was to the sea, and his name came from how he spent his days, as well as the location of his house, so close to the sea that winter storms often brought waves to his doorstep. Hugh gave thanks each day for his safe return to his family after a day of fishing and for the wondrous bounty of life that swam in the mysterious depths of the ocean. It was well known that he never took more than his fair share, and he had been seen to return fish when his nets were full. Hugh loved and feared and, above all, respected the power of the sea.

Hugh descended into a gully, a bay with high cliffs on either side known locally as a *geo*.[3] His strength and skills were required as he climbed down rocks and walked along a shore that, at low tide, was paved with stones descending in size from boulders at the farthest point to white pebbles inland. Hugh knew that a cave, always flooded at high tide, would be there for him to explore at this time of the early morning. As he maneuvered his way along the coast, his eyes adjusted to the otherworldly combination of sea mist, sunlight, and shadow.

Then he saw her.

---

1. SHEN-ack-as nah MY-cheen–VAR-ah
2. E-yawn nah MAH-rah
3. joe

Seated on a rock, with her back to Hugh, was a woman. Long, blonde hair cascaded to her waist, and she was dressed in a loosely woven white garment that billowed about her like moor fog. She seemed oblivious to Hugh's presence as she combed her hair and massaged her hands and feet. A few feet away from her, on another boulder, was a dark article that seemed to ripple like ocean waves. As Hugh crept closer, he could distinguish its shape of tail and fins, covered with ruby red scales, and in the center of each was a drop of golden light.

Hugh knew that the creature before him was "the damsel of the deep," a mermaid. And he knew the legend that said a mortal has power over a mermaid if he keeps her fish tail, for then she cannot return to her home of fish and coral but must stay in his earthly one.

The faery woman continued grooming herself, all the while gently singing a haunting tune about fishermen lost at sea. Hugh's mind was filled with questions that longed for answers from the mermaid. What is it like to swim with dolphins? Where do you sleep? Can you talk with fishes? Do you have children? How long do you live? What have you seen that humans never will? Is it true that you appear to a fisherman when he has been chosen to die? And because Hugh wanted to know the answer to the last question most of all, because he was the fisherman who could see her, he carefully worked his way toward the iridescent tail.

But walking on stones is neither easy nor quiet. The clatter of the pebbles beneath the man's feet gave the mermaid warning, and just as Hugh lunged for the fish garment, so did she. Both mortal and faery fingers grabbed at the tail, but it was the strength of Hugh's massive arms that allowed him to pull hard enough so that the scales slid through the mermaid's grasp, and Hugh clutched the slippery skin to his chest.

For a moment, the two remained crouched over the rock. The woman's blue eyes sparkled like jewels and seemed to pierce Hugh through and through. Slowly, she stood, tall and straight, and her height was equal to that of the man's. She was a queen among such simple creatures as humans, and her regal beauty of ivory skin, delicate features, and inner strength caused Hugh to feel he should fall to his knees before her and beg forgiveness for his rude behavior. But a desperate need to hear the answers to his questions kept him from handing back what was rightfully hers.

There was a long silence, and the differences of two worlds, between them. Finally, Hugh spoke.

"Do not be afraid. I only wish to . . ."

"Afraid? You think that I could be afraid of you? I am not. Mortal man, give me back the article you hold in your thieving hands."

Hugh looked down at the fish tail, then back at its owner. "I will not. At least, not until you answer my questions. Please, I am only curious."

"You presume to ask questions of me? I am the queen of the deep and the endless sea. Why should I satisfy your curiosity of me?"

"Because I mean you no harm. You are indeed a queen, and I am in awe of you and your beauty. But I am also a simple man who has been given this opportunity to speak with one from the faery world, a world we do not know or understand. And so I beg you, tell me of your world, and of your reason for being here, today. Tell me if your presence foretells a tragedy for me or family or friends."

The mermaid seemed amused by Hugh's fears, and her response was gentler in tone. "You are indeed a bold man. You disturbed me at my morning pleasures, and, indeed, you might have brought tragedy upon yourself. My anger could blast and wither you off this earth." She paused, waiting to see the effect of her words. Hugh neither moved nor answered. "Are you an honest man, as well as a brave one?"

"Aye, people have said so."

"Then do you give your word that you will return to me that which you now hold?"

"I have said so. I will return it in exchange for the answers to what I must know."

"You are reckless, mortal man. You must know how dangerous it is to try to understand our world that is one of mystery and bewildering truth. However, I have never spoken with a human before, and I am somewhat at your mercy. But only somewhat, *Eoghann na mara*." And the mermaid laughed with a deep, bubbling sound that chilled Hugh's heart. "You are surprised that I know your name. I know so many things. What is it that *you* want to know?"

Hugh wasted no time. "Only two things. Is it true that the appearance of a mermaid is the warning of a coming tragedy for the one who sees her? And what is it like, the world beneath the waves?"

The mermaid gazed long into Hugh's brown eyes. In the play of shadow and light, she seemed to shimmer before him, and he began to wonder if she would disappear into the mist. But finally she sat down upon her boulder again and motioned for him to sit upon the rock that once held her amphibious skin.

"I am well aware," said the mermaid, "that you consider us your mortal enemy because we are supposed to be the harbingers of disaster, the forecasters of death at sea. But let me tell you that this message we bring is as painful for us to bear as it is for you to receive. We know the secret plans of the god of the boundless deep, but we are powerless to change his whim when he chooses one here, or a ship full there, to die. All that we can do is to swim at once to the vicinity of the tragedy in hopes that the people will be able to save themselves and others. We are thought to be evil beings, but in fact what we do is done out of sympathy and pity for you humans."

"And today?" asked Hugh. "Are you here, in this bay, to bring such a warning?"

The mermaid smiled. "No, *Eoghann na Mara*. I am glad to inform you that I am here only for my own pleasure. I give you no warnings today."

Then it was Hugh who laughed. The mermaid seemed startled by the loud relief expressed in his laughter, but she waited, amused, until he was quiet again.

"Now, I have given you the answer to the first of your questions. As to the second, I am afraid I cannot give you that one." Hugh stared at the faery woman, a look of disappointment on his weather-beaten face. His hands glided over the iridescent scales of the mermaid's tail, and he listened patiently as she tried to explain.

"Your desire to know more about myself and my world is a desire that cannot be satisfied, for our world is beyond the realm of human understanding or knowledge. It is impossible for me to explain in your language what it is like to be a faery, on earth or in the sea. But this I can say. I live in a kingdom of grandeur and beauty beyond your imagination. The elements that are so cruel to you—wind, rain, lightning, storms—only serve to increase the majesty and power of our world by creating mountains and valleys or by decorating them with jewels and gems. I see creatures that are beyond description with their wondrous forms, and I am surrounded by colors you will never know. And the human qualities that bring you such pain—greed, selfishness, anger, old age—are unknown within our world."

"And is there death?" asked Hugh.

"Yes, there is. But our natural death, which comes after many more years than any human can comprehend, is not one of suffering, but one of gentle passage into light. We do not know fear or sadness. We know only the infinite wonder of magic."

For a long time after the mermaid had said all that she could say, Hugh sat silently gazing out to sea. Then, without a request from either the human or the faery, they both stood and looked at each other.

"Thank you," said Hugh. "Most sincerely, I thank you. If it were possible, I would visit your kingdom, but it will have to be your beautiful and generous words that bring me the happiness that is possible only in my imagination." Hugh reached out with his hands, and placed the red and golden garment in the mermaid's outstretched arms.

"Son of man, I admire your honesty. I am glad to have met one who is worthy of remembering my words. And now I shall reward you for your courage. At each new moon, just before dawn, come to the top of the cliff where you will find a faery stone that points to the sky. There you will find a supply of fish that will support you and your family until the next new moon. The only conditions are these: No one but yourself may come for the fish, and no one but yourself may know my story until you have passed your eightieth winter. Only then may you tell what you have heard."

Hugh nodded his head in agreement, then turned and walked away. He knew, without asking, that their conversation was ended and that her transformation was not for him to see.

Eoghann na mara kept his promise, as did the queen of the sea. In the early morning of each new moon, Hugh found a supply of fish beside the stone that pointed to the sky. When he passed his eightieth birthday he gathered together his children and grandchildren and told them the story of the mermaid. Three months later, he died, knowing no fear but only a welcoming of the light.

Songs

The Mermaid's Croon

Cronan na Maighdinn-Mhara[1]

This song was recorded from the singing of Penny O'Henley of South Uist. It is a lullaby sung by a mermaid who was married to a mortal and now sings to their child. The following note from Marjory Kennedy-Fraser and Kenneth Macleod explains the symbolism of the animals:

> The Swan is "the daughter of the twelve moons," the seals are "the children of the King of Lochlann under spells," and the Mallard is under the Virgin's protection; hence all three are "sacred," and not even reivers [thieves; the word means "stolen"] would meddle with the "tenderling" left under such protection. (Songs of the Hebrides, p. 153)

Sleep beneath the foam o' the waves,
On reefs of sleep,
Dreaming in dew-mist.
Sleep beneath the foam o' the waves,
On reefs of sleep,
Dreaming in dew-mist.
Thy sea-bed the seals o'er-head,
From reivers dread securely guarding.
Seals o'er-head thy deep sea-bed,
From reivers dread securely guarding.
Ho! mo nigh'n dubh[2]
He! mo nigh'n dubh

Mo nighean dubh
Stu mo chuachag[3].
He! mo nigh'n dubh
Ho! mo nigh'n dubh
Mo nighean dubh,
Stu mo chuachag.
While I croon, white swan of the moon,
Wild duck of the sound,
By thee are resting.
Moon white swan, white swan of the moon,
Wild duck of the sound,
A-near thee resting.

---

1. KROW-nan nah MY-cheen–VAR-ah
2. nian du
3. chuachak

The Mermaid's Croon

Part II—The Faery Folk of the Water

Lady of the Lake

INTRODUCTION

I chose to include this story for one simple reason—it haunted me. It is Welsh, which is part of my maternal heritage, and it is about a member of the faery world. But more than that it is about love, and how one (mortal) can view it as eternal, while the other (faery) perceives it as limited and defined. What haunts me is that this happens in our world all too often, and the punishment for the one whose heart is broken because he or she did not understand the rules is often more painful than even time can heal.

But that is what stories are all about. They give us a chance to understand ourselves and to feel comfortable in the company of those who have lived with similar pain. That is why the same stories appear throughout the world, their only differences being the location and/or characters. The trials, the soul-searching, the triumphs, and the losses are the same. Mortal or faery, we all suffer.

Lady of the Lake

Gwraig Annwn[1]

The grey old man in the corner,
Of his father heard a story,
Which from his father he had heard,
And after them I have remembered.

My sons were healers. They were known as the Physicians of Myddfai, and they were the beginning of many generations dedicated to ending pain and misery in the lives of humans. They were unrivaled in their knowledge of the medicinal powers of plants and herbs, and their skills made them famous throughout Wales and beyond.

I am their father. I knew nothing of medicine, and the only skill I taught my sons was that of tending cattle. I was a herdsman, plain and simple, and I am not remembered. Except for the fact that I was married to her.

I am glad to be forgotten. My sons will keep alive what is important. The rest is just a story, a story of youth and love, promises and mistakes, mortal and faery. And yet, like all stories, mine deserves to be told, so that those who come after can remember and learn.

My mother was a widow, and I was not just her only son but also her only child. My father died during the struggles when the princes of South Wales were fighting to preserve the independence of their homeland. My mother and I were left with no understanding, which brought us much sorrow, and a herd of cattle that increased and prospered, which brought us some comfort. As I grew to manhood, my days were spent with cows and bulls, yet, like all men, I longed for a companion to love, someone who would give me sons and a hand to hold while we slept.

---

1. gwrag a-NOON

My mother did the best that she could to ease my loneliness by filling the long, dark nights with stories. It was from her that I learned about the *Gwragedd Annwn*,[2] the Welsh water faeries, beautiful lake maidens who search for mortals to be their husbands. I heard the legends of towns below the waters of the lakes, and how towers and battlements can be seen beneath the surface of the water, and sometimes bells can be heard. She told me about a rock that holds a door; those who dare to enter will find themselves on an island that remains invisible to those who are not so brave. The island is inhabited by the *Gwragedd Annwn*, and they will feed you and give you much pleasure, as long as you do not remove anything from their faery world.

You see, the faery folk have rules. And if a rule is broken, whether by accident or misunderstanding, the consequences are terrible and forever. I hope someday my sons will understand and forgive a man who was foolish because he thought love was stronger than any rule.

My story begins on a day like any other, when I was in search of cattle that had strayed. In my quest, I climbed to the top of a hill, from which I could see the shores and clear waters of *Llyn y Fan Fach*.[3] The lake was absolutely still; there was no movement or sound, as if time had stopped and was waiting for permission to continue. I remember wondering, briefly, where I should search next, for I saw no sign of the missing cows. And then, I, too, was frozen in silence, when I saw her.

She was beautiful to me beyond all words. Dark hair fell over her shoulders, and she was arranging it into ringlets, using her long fingers as a comb and the glassy surface of the lake as a mirror. Her dress was all shades of blue, and her skin was as white as sea foam. I was so struck by her grace and beauty that it was several minutes before I realized she was sitting on the water, and I knew there were no rocks to support her.

She was *Gwraig Annwn*, a Lady of the Lake. And I was immediately in love.

When she finally looked at me I moved closer, until I was standing on the edge of the lake. All I could think of was that I wanted to give her something, something that would make her realize how much I wanted her to stay. So I offered her the only thing I carried with me, a loaf of barley bread and a block of cheese given to me by my mother that morning.

---

2. GWRA-geth a-NOON
3. hleen uh vahn vahkh

I stood for a long while with my hands outstretched, before finally she began to glide toward me. I was overjoyed as she approached and then was immediately filled with grief when she shook her head at my offerings and turned away from me. I reached for her, but she cried out, "Hard baked is thy bread! 'Tis not easy to catch me." Then she dove under the water and was gone.

When I returned home that evening, I did not bring the cattle, but only a heart filled with longing. I told my mother what I had seen and heard, and I begged her to remember all that she knew from the stories so I would know what to offer the Lady to keep her with me.

"There must have been a spell that kept her from taking the hard-baked bread," said my mother. "Tomorrow, take unbaked dough in your pocket, and see if that will do."

The next morning, before there was sunlight to guide me, I left our house and set off toward *Llyn y Fan Fach*, with dough in my pocket and hope in my heart. I stood beside the shore as long as my legs would hold me and then sat, waiting and waiting and waiting more. Hours passed. I listened to the birds as they greeted the day and felt the sun hot on my back in the afternoon and watched the shadows grow dim as evening approached. I had all but given up for that day, knowing I would return the next, when she appeared, even more beautiful than I remembered. I held out my hands, one filled with dough and the other reaching to hold the Lady's hand. I offered her my love, but she refused it all, saying, "Unbaked is thy bread! I will not have thee." She dove under the water and was gone.

But this time I saw a smile upon her face, and I believed it to be a smile of promise. The next morning I left our home before sunrise again, with pockets full of bread that was soft and only slightly baked. I spent another long day waiting beside the lake. I remember seeing my mother's cattle straying among the rocks, and I knew I should be tending to them. I remember rain falling and thinking I should seek shelter somewhere. But I would not leave, for fear of missing her arrival and my third chance.

Late in the afternoon I saw a strange and wondrous thing that brought hope back into my thoughts. Several cows were walking along the surface of the waters, and I waited anxiously to see if they were messengers of her arrival. Indeed, they were, for soon the Lady reappeared, lovelier than ever. I rushed out into the water, and she glided toward me, a smile upon her face and her hand outstretched to receive the bread I offered. I asked her to be my wife, and she agreed.

Then she made a curious remark. "I will live together with you until you strike me three blows without a cause, *tri ergyd diachos*.[4] If that should happen, I will leave you forever."

At that moment, it is true, I would have agreed to anything, for all I desired was to marry her. I could not believe I would ever give her even one causeless blow, and so I readily gave my promise and accepted this rule.

If you can imagine how incredibly happy I was at that moment, then perhaps you can also imagine how distressed I was when she withdrew her hand from mine, turned, and dove under the water. My grief was so sudden and so deep that I could think of nothing else but to follow her. I knew I would die, but I did not care. Before I could act on these morbid thoughts, there arose from out of the lake two beautiful ladies, identical to each other and identical to the one who had accepted my proposal of marriage. They were accompanied by a man who can only be described as ancient in appearance yet youthful in strength. His hair and beard were white, and his face was covered with the lines of many years and much knowledge. His arms and legs were solid, as if carved from the oak tree, and his sea-green eyes pierced through my own and into my heart.

Yet when he spoke his voice was gentle and soothing. "You have proposed to marry one of my daughters, and I consent to this union, if you can determine which of my daughters is the one you love."

This was no easy task, for the two were as alike as two white doves. It seemed quite impossible to choose which one was to be my bride, and again I was filled with the grief of losing, after believing I had won just a brief moment ago. I looked at the two lovely maidens, searching for anything that would give me a clue, and was about to give up in despair, when one of them moved her foot forward ever so slightly. The motion was simple, but I also knew it was intentional, and so I chose her.

"You have chosen rightly," said her father. "Be a kind and faithful husband, and I will give her, as a dowry, as many sheep, cattle, goats, and horses as she can count without stopping for a breath. But remember, if you prove unkind to her, and strike her three times without cause, *tri ergyd diachos*, she and her dowry shall return to me."

This was the rule, and I readily agreed, believing it to be an easy one to follow, and believing, as I said before, that love was stronger than any rule. I did not know that faeries do not forgive the mistakes of humans.

---

4. tree AIR-geed dee-AH-khose

My bride was not only beautiful; she also was clever. When her dowry of sheep, goats, horses, and cattle began to appear from under the water, she counted in fives until her breath was exhausted. When she was done, the number of livestock we now owned was more than I had ever thought possible in one lifetime. We were married and knew only happiness and prosperity for several years. Perhaps the greatest joys of all were the three sons she gave me.

I wish I could tell you that this is the end of my story and that the mother of my sons continues to hold my hand as we sleep, side by side. But it is not so, for she was faery and I was mortal, and sometimes the two are so different that even love is not strong enough to keep them together. And it was never that I forgot the rule or disregarded it. It was simply because of our differences.

The first occasion was a christening to which we had been invited. The parents of the child were close friends of ours, and I was anxious and delighted to attend. But my wife refused, saying that the distance was too great for her to walk. I knew this not to be true, for we had walked it before. Yet she insisted it was too far. So I asked her if she would be willing to fetch one of her horses from the field where it grazed and ride it to the christening. "I will," she replied, "if you will bring me my gloves which I left in the house." When I returned from this errand, I discovered she had not gone for the horse, and I knew we would be too late to make leaving worthwhile if we did not hasten. So, without thinking, I took one of the gloves, gently slapped my wife upon the shoulder with it, and said, "Go! Go, or we will miss the celebration."

The stillness that followed my action was as dark and as deep as the hour before dawn. My wife turned to me and said, "I do not wish to attend this foolish celebration. The poor babe is entering a world of sin and sorrow; misery lies before it. Why should we celebrate?" My protests and explanations did not matter to her, and we did not attend the christening.

Time passed, and the incident, for me, was forgotten.

Several years later we were at a wedding. Except for our own, this was the first ceremony of marriage between mortals that she had witnessed. The bride was young and fair; the groom was old, toothless, and miserly. My wife was strangely quiet during the exchange of vows, and her eyes remained downcast, staring at her folded hands. Later, when the room was filled with the sounds of laughter and the calls of congratulations, I was horrified to see her cover her face with her hands and then burst into tears, crying most pitifully, as if her heart could not bear such grief. "What is wrong with you?" I asked, as I pulled her hands away.

And there it was again—the long stillness, the staring into my eyes, and the shaking of her head. She spoke dreadful words to me. "Truth is wedded to age for greed, and not for love. Summer and winter cannot agree. I know these people are entering into trouble, and I know that your trouble has begun as well, for now you have struck me a second time without cause. Be careful."

This time, the incident was not forgotten. I *was* careful, fully realizing now that the rule would be interpreted, rewarded, or punished according to faery law. My mortality was no defense.

Years passed on. I was a blessed and lucky man. Never a day passed by that I did not give thanks for the love shared between my wife and me. Our sons grew into particularly fine men and left our home to pursue their own careers and families. In the midst of so much happiness I almost forgot that which I most needed to remember.

And then my mother died. She left this world suddenly, and I was unprepared for the darkness of my grief. At the funeral, I hoped to be comforted by my wife. But much to my dismay and embarrassment, she seemed to be in the happiest of spirits, laughing and singing tunes that were much too merry for this sad occasion. I was so shocked that I stopped her by grabbing her shoulders and shaking her once. "Hush, my love! What is wrong with you?"

When there is a moment in your life that changes everything, a moment when all that was good is suddenly and eternally gone, it is difficult to identify exactly when it was that you truly understood. Was it when I placed my hand on her shoulder that I knew? Or when she looked at me with such sorrow in her eyes? Or when she whispered, "Farewell"? I watched as she walked away from me and out across the meadow, knowing there was nothing I could say and that she was lost to me forever.

What I did the rest of that day, that week, that month, that year, is known only to the echoes that haunt the Black Mountains and to the shadows that are seen beneath the waters of *Llyn y Fan Fach*.

I survived. I kept the memory of my wife with me by talking about her with my sons. They often wandered the rocks and fields close to the lake, hoping that their mother would appear once more. And then, one day, as they rambled in the valley now called *Cwm Meddygon*,[5] she was suddenly there, and in her hands was a box. She admonished the young men, scolding them for their selfishness. "You are to be healers of mankind," she told them, "and this box contains all the medicines and instructions you will ever need for the preservation of health." She promised she would return whenever her counsel was most needed, and then she vanished.

---

5. koom meth-UH-gone

Our sons, Cadogan, Gruffydd, and Einion, are indeed great physicians. They are known as the *Meddygon Myddfai*,[6] the Physicians of Myddfai, and I am sure their sons and their grandsons will follow them as healers. They tell me that their mother has met them near the banks of the lake on several occasions and teaches them about the medicinal qualities of the plants and herbs that grow in the Black Mountains. She remains young and beautiful, say my sons, and expresses her love for them in many ways.

My sons also say that she has never spoken of me.

---

6. meth-UH-gone MUHTH-vie

Author Heather McNeil enjoying the beauty of the ocean and moors.

Castlebay, Isle of Barra.

John Allen MacNeil, the boatman and guardian of Kisimul Castle.

The Great Hall of Kisimul Castle.

The Macneil
crest and
original
tartan.

Kisimul Castle, the home and stronghold of the Macneils of
Barra since A.D. 1030.

Kirsty MacKay, teller of "The Changeling Child."

Ronnie Boyd, teller of "The Baker and the Faeries."

Annie MacKinnon.

Calum MacNeil, an expert on the history of the Clan Macneil and descendant of the original chiefs.

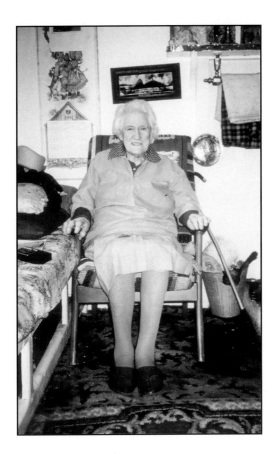

Morag MacAulay, the "Fair Maid of Barra."

On the boat with Roddy Nicholson (left) and Jimmy Campbell (right).

Author Heather McNeil raking cockles on Cocklestrand Beach, which, at low tide, doubles as an air strip.

Celtic crosses mark the graves of priests at Cille Bharra Cemetery.

The ghosts of three dead sailors are said to haunt this house.

The rocky coast of Barra where the seals and the waves play.

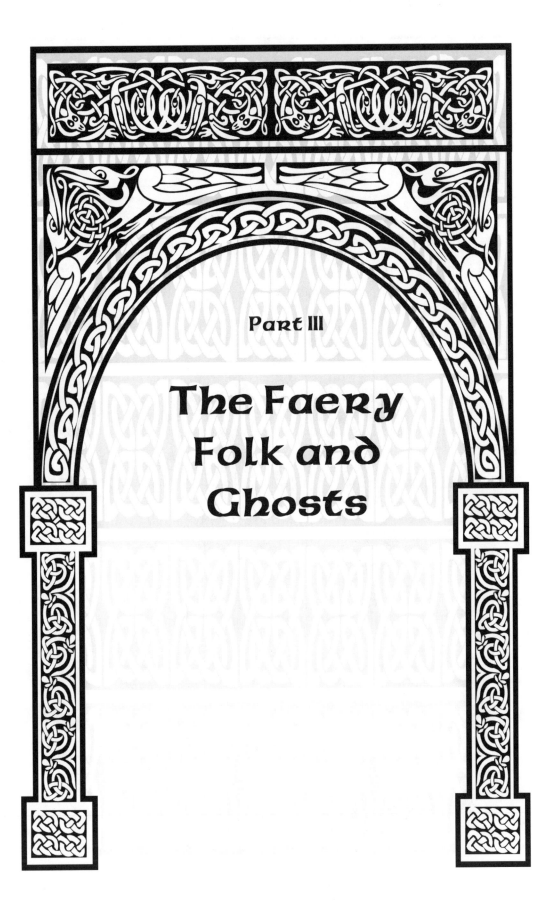

Part III

The Faery Folk and Ghosts

nancy chien-eriksen

The Sea Claims Her Own

INTRODUCTION

While I was visiting the land of my ancestors, Mary Sarah MacNeil and I walked the shores of the Isle of Vatersay one sunlit October morning. The island is almost abandoned, with only a handful of people still living there. The beaches are rocky, the land is flat, and the sea can be seen or heard from almost anywhere.

Two objects that we came across have stayed in my memory as strong reminders of the powerful forces that can change history and family. The first was the shell of a land mine, left behind after World War II to rust in the mist and rain of Vatersay. It is harmless now, but it had been planted on the island to harm many in an instant.

The second was a memorial, built to commemorate the lives of 450 people who died on board the *Annie Jane*, an emigrant ship that wrecked on the west beach in 1853. Many of the dead were islanders, perhaps forced to leave their homes during the Highland Clearances, when land-owners preferred the profits they could make from sheep to that of having crofters (farmers) or fishermen on their land. One can only imagine the terror of that night, as men, women, and children cried out in the darkness and "the sea claimed her own."

Kenneth Macleod, in his poetic book, *The Road to the Isles: Poetry, Lore, and Tradition of the Hebrides*, mentions an oral tale passed down by the people of North Uist that haunted me with its vivid image of ancient Vikings who return from their watery graves. That image became the next story, another tale of how we are always at the mercy of the relentless power of the sea.

The Sea Claims Her Own

Dhiarr a' Mhuir a Bhith ga Tadhal[1]

In the Hebrides, the Sea is life. She opens her womb, and releases Her children, both strange and wonderful, that are food to the fishermen and their families. Her blood ebbs and flows with the tides of the moon, rising to send ships safely home to their harbors or pulling away to reveal the creatures that live beneath her ivory skirts of sand. She is the lullaby that soothes the wailing child and the ballad that brings a sailor home to his sweetheart. Her gentle touch is left behind in colors of emerald and aquamarine and pearl.

In the Hebrides, the Sea is death. From Her belly, She releases storms of anger and greed. Her blood boils with rage, and She tosses the ships and boats that annoy Her simply because they exist. She selfishly pulls into Her arms the bodies of those She desires and jealously holds them in their eternal rest. And when the body of one whose life She has taken is taken from Her, She hurls Herself upon the shore with cries and crashes of fury. Then Her touch is cold, and Her colors are the deepest indigo and grey and black of precious life that is taken away without fairness or caring.

The Sea claims Her own.

The body of a sailor was washed up onto the shore of North Uist. Purple bruises colored his arms and legs, for he had been tossed hard upon rocks and between waves. But somehow his face had remained untouched, and the villagers looked down upon the handsome youth with sorrow for the family who would be missing him that night, and relief that he was not one of their own. One young woman, whose husband had been lost at sea not so long ago, knelt beside the seaman and gently brushed the long, black hair away from his brow. She closed the empty, blue eyes and held his cold hands, remembering the warm touch of the one she had loved so dearly but who was lost forever in the endless depths of the ocean.

---

1. yeer ah voor ah vee gah tahl

"What shall we do with him?" someone asked.

"Bury him," another replied.

The silence of agreement followed, and then the villagers lifted the youth onto their shoulders to carry him away from the sand and onto soil, where his grave would be dug.

"Put him back."

The villagers stopped their procession and turned to see who had spoken. It was an old woman, her back turned to them and her withered face gazing out to where sky and sea touched. "He belongs to the Sea," she declared, "and the Sea claims Her own. Put him back."

"No!" The young widow cried out, and pushed her way through the crowd. "He should be buried, where I—we—can visit him and share our prayers."

"He is not your husband. He is not ours to mourn," said the old woman, her grey eyes staring into the green ones of the girl. "Why do you think Mother Ocean storms and floods our islands? She is angry when we keep the bodies of those she wanted. Give him back to her."

"No. The Sea has already taken his life; surely She will give us his body."

The old woman turned and walked away. "She will not."

The villagers watched as the woman disappeared into the mist. "You must not listen to her," pleaded the widow. "What she says is not truth but stories told by the elders as they amuse themselves around the fire. Think of your own loved ones who have only the fishes and crabs to visit them. Would you not rather be able to put flowers on their graves and loving words on the stones that mark those graves? Would you not?"

The villagers knew that they would, as they remembered sons and brothers and husbands whose absence haunted their days. So, without another word, they carried the body of the sailor across the sand and rocks, and they buried him in the ancient Temple of the Trinity, so far from the Sea that She could not hold him or sing to him or even see the mound of earth that was his blanket of eternal rest.

Islanders came and went, leaving behind bouquets of heather or words spoken only in their hearts. By the time of twilight, the widow remained alone beside the grave, mourning the brief life of the young man and remembering another. When her tears and prayers were ended, she began the long and lonely walk home to her cottage by the sea. But as she traveled the path that followed the shore, she saw a ship gliding into the bay. It was a dark ship, with black sails and masts, and she saw no one at the prow. Yet the barge never faltered, slipping quietly into the harbor with its sails wide and open, although there was no wind.

Then from off the ghostly ship stepped three men, all of them tall, with hair like gold, as the Vikings of the old stories. Without a word they walked onto the shore, past the widow who could not seem to move or speak, and along the path that led into the Temple of the Trinity. The woman watched in horror as the golden-haired giants knelt next to the fresh-dug grave and, with their hands, pulled and clawed away the earth until the sailor's body was revealed to them. They lifted him out of his grave and onto their shoulders and then silently retraced their steps out of the Temple, along the path, across the beach, and onto the ship. Suddenly, without a breath of wind, the sails flew wide and full, and the ship pulled away from the shore.

The widow watched the phantom ship and its ghostly crew glide soundlessly to where the sky touches the sea. When it had disappeared into the fire of the setting sun, she turned to walk home, trying to understand what she alone had seen.

But she was not alone. Standing behind her was the old woman. The two gazed into each other's eyes in silence for a long while, one face creased with many years of sorrow and loss, the other still bearing the traces of tears. Finally, the elder reached out, gently brushed the other's cheek, and walked away, her words drifting behind her, until the younger could not distinguish the words from the wind.

"The Sea claims Her own. The Sea claims Her own. The Sea claims Her own."

Songs

The Sea Sorrow

Am Bron Mara[1]

This song was written down from the singing of Mary Macdonald on Mingulay and is a form of wailing chant well known in the Isles. Songs such as this one were the expressions of a woman's grief over the death of her loved one, yet such sorrow was believed to be cruel to the ones who drowned. "It is not right . . . to disturb the rest of the ones-no-more; it is bad enough to put sorrow on them, but it is seven times worse to put anger on them" (Kennedy-Fraser and Macleod, p. 114). It was considered wrong to sing a drowning-song twice in one evening, and some of the elders refused to sing such a tune after sunset. There were stories that the spirits of the drowned ones would become so exasperated that they would haunt those who excessively mourned their death, causing the women such a fright that their tears would quickly end. The Land-under-waves was not such a terrible place to spend eternity, said those who lived there. "I have the best heroes of Lochlann beside me . . . and the best bards of Erin, and the best storytellers of Alba, and what we do not know ourselves, the seal and the swan tell us" (Kennedy-Fraser and Macleod, p. 114).

But the women who are left behind still grieve and remember. And the Sea claims Her own.

Mouth of gladness! Music's laughter,
Sad that I am not beside thee.
Hu io ho hug o[2]
On ridge of ocean, shelf of shore,
What place so e'er the tide has left thee
Hu io ho hug o
Side by side, my love, dear heart,
Side by side nor thought to part.
Ever quiet to sleep a falling,
Croon of waves, o love, our tala.[3]

Hu io ho hug o
Ah! My wound! He hears no more,
Wave-drown'd is my cry of woe.
Mouth of gladness! Music's laughter!
Sad that I am not beside thee.
Hu io ho hug o
Hear'st not my cry now?

---

1. ahm brawn MAH-rah
2. hoo yo ho hook o
3. lulling song

The Sea Sorrow

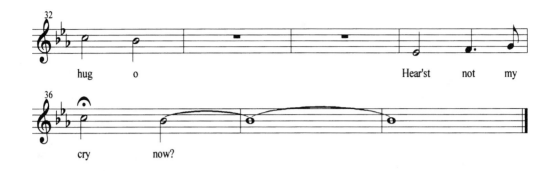

hug   o   Hear'st   not   my

cry   now?

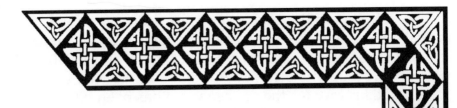

The Buried Moon

INTRODUCTION

This is a haunting story I have told for many years. The images of good versus evil and beauty versus beast captivated me when I first read it and led me to research as many versions of this Welsh folktale as I could find. Then I created my own version, weaving together bits and pieces from other retellings, plus adding my own, until the story rested comfortably inside my head and heart.

That is how stories are born and why storytellers feel so passionate about the stories they tell. There are blood, sweat, and fears behind each original touch, plus the talent to choose what is best for you from the skeleton of the original and let go of what isn't. I tell beginning storytellers that there is no right way or wrong way to tell a story. But the story must be your own creation, born from your own unique talents and gifts. It must also be a true rendering of the original, and the teller must have knowledge about its history and the people whose breath first gave it life.

My maternal grandfather's ancestors were Welsh. "Bapop," as we called him, was the first storyteller in my life, and I remember clearly his tall tales, recitations from Shakespeare and cowboy poetry, and beautiful vocalizations of Scottish ballads. He was a masterful entertainer, and his love for the spoken word has been passed down through all the generations that followed. He was Santa Claus, Laurence Olivier, and a circus barker all rolled into one wonderful grandfather.

Tell the stories. The children, and their children's children, will remember.

The Buried Moon

Claddedigaith y Lleuad[1]

Try to imagine the night without the Moon. Not just a few nights, but forever, no moon. And now imagine, in that darkness, the strange and horrible creatures that live there. Bogles, with long, leathery noses and a fondness for pinching. Gwyllion, who enjoy sitting among the rocks and silently watching, but not helping, lost travelers. Kelpies, who take on the form of horses and then take their innocent riders for a deadly ride into the bog. Will-o'-the-Wisps, who dance ahead of lost travelers with lanterns tied to their backs, leading the humans farther and farther away from the path. Hags, who are worse than witches because they eat their victims. These are the creatures who come out during the dark of the moon to terrify and destroy.

When the Moon shines, these Horrors wait, and the marshes and bogs are filled only with the scuttlings of lizards and snakes, the screeching of owls, and the sudden flapping of leathery bat wings. The Moon's light reveals the deathtraps of mud holes and black pools, and a traveler is able to safely find his way home.

But when the Moon does not shine, out come the Things that live in darkness, scratching and screeching, howling and haunting. Their human victims, exhausted with the fear that causes them to run blindly and stumble painfully, never see the rising sun. It is during the Dark of the Moon that death is the most fearsome.

Long ago, the Moon came to hear about these Terrors, and she was troubled. She decided to find out for herself if it was true that the ancient Evil ruled whenever she rested. So she wrapped herself in a long, black cloak, and she hid her yellow, shining hair in the hood. Only her bare feet glowed gently as she glided down out of the sky and into the bog.

---

1. klah-theh-DEE-geith uh HLEI-ahd

The Moon looked all about her. She saw pools of black water that seemed to reflect no light and great black snags that the mind could twist into horrible and grisly forms. She saw mounds of mud that she knew could suck down and suffocate human or animal, and as she thought about these deathtraps, she realized she was not alone. At first there were only whispers—"The Moon! It's the Moon!" Then, suddenly, there was a scream, and the Moon saw the glowing eyes of Black Annis, the witch who eats children. She saw dead folk rising out of the water, their empty eye sockets blood red and blazing with fire. She saw white hands beckoning her to follow, and she saw the Evil Eye staring at her from the deepest part of the dark. Bony fingers poked at her, foul odors filled the air, and some Thing twined itself around her neck and slithered down her back.

The Moon knew these were the Creatures of Fear, and she would not allow herself to be their prey. She stepped lightly as a summer wind from tuft to tuft between the gurgling water holes, with only the flickering light of her feet to guide her. She sang quietly about gentle warm breezes and the light of a thousand stars. Suddenly, there was another light ahead—a Will-o'-the-Wisp? The Moon glanced at the light shimmering and fading, and, in that moment, her foot slipped. With both hands she grabbed at a snag of peat to keep from falling into the black pool, but as soon as she touched it, the snag came to life and wrapped itself around her wrists, gripping her so tightly she could not escape. The Moon pulled and twisted and fought, but she was held fast, and there was nothing but Evil all around her. "The Moon!" whispered the Horrors in the darkness. "We've got the Moon!"

After a long and terrifying while, the Moon heard another sound, a voice calling and calling for help. "I will not answer," thought the Moon. "It is only a trick, and if I believe it to be real then I give it power." But the voice continued, sobbing and crying, and then there was a scream of pure terror, followed by the sound of running footsteps and someone slipping and falling into the mud. "Help!" cried the voice. "Please help me! Is anyone there?"

It was a boy, a stranger to the bog, who had strayed on the moor and was now being tormented by all the Evil that lived there. Every terrifying story he had ever heard had come to life in the bog. Every bad deed he had ever done threatened him with eternal life in hell, and every selfish thought he had ever kept hidden now tortured him with slimy fingers that stroked his cheek and chattering teeth that bit his hands.

The Moon saw that the boy was stumbling nearer and nearer to the bottomless, black pool. She was so angry at being helpless and so sorry for what she knew would be the innocent boy's death, that she struggled even harder to break free. As she twisted and turned, the hood fell back from her shining yellow hair, and the light drove away the darkness.

The boy cried for joy and began running out of the swamp in such a hurry that he scarcely glanced at the light that streamed across the water at his feet. In moments he was gone, and the Moon was left alone. She fought against the snag in fury and madness, until, exhausted, she sank to her knees. As the Moon knelt in the bog, she bowed her head. The hood fell back over her hair, and the light was gone.

Immediately, the Creatures of Fear returned, screeching and howling with delight. "Damn you!" yelled the Hags. "Damn you for spoiling our spells."

"Damn you for keeping us in our coffins at night," moaned the Dead.

"We'll poison her," shrieked the Hags.

"We'll strangle her," whispered the Dead, and they plucked at her throat with cold fingers.

"We'll drown her, bury her, smother her!" Each of the Horrors demanded the privilege of killing the Moon in its own horrible way, and they argued her fate throughout the night until a faint light glowed in the east. When they realized they would not have the time to do their worst, bones and teeth caught hold of the Moon and pulled her into the water. The Dead trampled her into the slime and held her down while Bogles found a huge stone to roll on top of her. Then all the Evils fled into their dark corners and coffins, leaving two Will-o'-the-Wisps to watch over the Moon and make sure that she stayed, buried, under the rock.

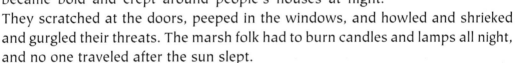

Days passed, and it became time for the light of the Moon to erase the dark. But the nights remained dark and evil, and the creatures that once were found only in the bog became bold and crept around people's houses at night. They scratched at the doors, peeped in the windows, and howled and shrieked and gurgled their threats. The marsh folk had to burn candles and lamps all night, and no one traveled after the sun slept.

Finally, the folk went to the wise woman who lived in the old mill and asked her if she could find the Moon. She looked in the cauldron bubbling with herbs. She stared at her reflection in a crooked mirror, and she read her book, but all she saw was darkness. "I don't understand," she muttered. "It's all dark and dead out there. I will think about this, but if any of you hear of anything or remember a clue, come by and tell me. Until we do find her, be sure to put a pinch of salt, a straw, and a button on the doorstep each night so the Horrors will not cross it."

They did as she told them. They talked and wondered among themselves at home, at the inn, and on the road. They tried to imagine or remember what had happened. And so it was that a young boy finally recalled his frightening journey through the bog many weeks ago. "I know where the Moon is!" he cried out to his parents as they huddled around a peat fire one evening. He described what had happened to him and said, "Just when I thought there wasn't a chance for me, this light shone out, soft and white, like the Moon. I didn't really look to see where it was coming from, but I do remember water, and a large black snag."

The next day the people returned to the Wise Woman, and the boy told her what he had remembered. She listened, and she stared into the cauldron and the mirror and the book. Then she nodded. "The bravest and the strongest must do as I tell you just before night falls. Each put a stone in your mouth and take a hazel twig in your hand. Say never a word until you are safely home again. Make your way into the middle of the marsh and look for a coffin, a candle, and a cross. Then you won't be far from your Moon."

The folk doubted her. "But where will we find her, old woman? How could there be a coffin, a candle, and a cross in the bog? Which of us must go? And what about the Horrors?"

The Wise Woman stamped her foot. "It is your fear that is keeping you here, babbling and trembling. If you do not like my advice, then stay at home and live without your Moon. Now, BE GONE!"

The next night at twilight, the folk went out together, all of them, including the boy. Each mouth held a pebble, and each hand held a hazel twig. No one spoke. The farther into the bog they walked, the more the air around them thickened with whispers and sighs. Wings and claws and teeth and the smell of rotting flesh were everywhere, but the people did not stop walking and they did not speak a word.

All at once the boy stopped next to a pool. Everyone saw the great stone, half in, half out of the water, like a granite coffin, and at the head of the tomb was the black snag, stretching out its two arms like a gruesome cross. The folk knelt down in the mud, crossed themselves, and silently said the Lord's Prayer, first forward because of the cross and then backward to keep the Evils away. Then they took hold of the stone and pulled it out of the mud and slime.

For one brief, amazing moment, they saw a beautiful face looking up at them, a face surrounded by shining yellow hair and deep black water. And then Lady Moon rose above the waters and the trees and the people, drifting in slow majesty, until she hung above them all, white and strong and so very bright. The Horrors howled and moaned, crawling and slithering back to their dark corners and coffins. The marsh folk returned with light hearts, and as soon as they were safely home, they told the story, again and again, grandparent to parent to child, and on again. And while the story is being told around the peat fire, the Moon lights the safe paths, and the lonely paths, that we all walk to this very day.

Songs

The Wind on the Moor

Null a Mhonadh e Nall a Mhonadh[1]

Marjory Kennedy-Fraser recorded this air from the singing of Marion Macleod on the Isle of Eigg.

Moorland winds a-moaning eerily,
Moorland winds a-wander.
Moorland winds a-moaning eerily,
Moorland winds out yonder.
Thro' the bogland faring wearily,
Thro' the bog I wander.
Fire-light, Love-light,
Bare, I wander.
Fire-light, Love-light,
Seeking I wander.
Moorland winds aye moaning eerily,
Moorland winds out yonder.
Thro' the bogland faring wearily,
Thro' the bog I wander.
Moorland winds a-blowing eerily,
Moorland winds out yonder.
Thro' the bogland faring wearily,
Thro' the bog I wander.
Fire-light, love-light,
Bare, I wander.
Fire-light, love-light,
Craving I wander.
Moorland winds a-blowing eerily,
Moorland winds out yonder.

---

1. nool ah VOHN-uh eh naul ah VOHN-uh

The Wind on the Moor

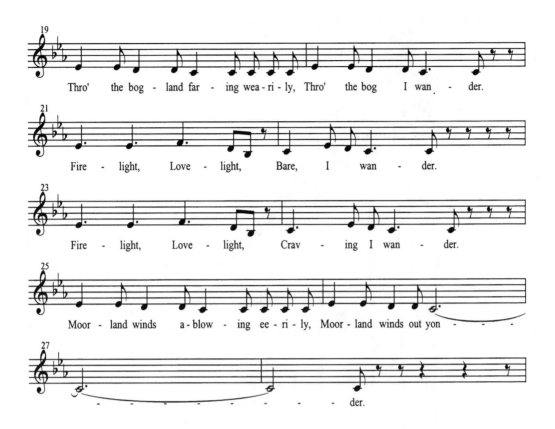

Thro' the bog - land far - ing wea - ri - ly, Thro' the bog I wan - der.

Fire - light, Love - light, Bare, I wan - der.

Fire - light, Love - light, Crav - ing I wan - der.

Moor - land winds a - blow - ing ee - ri - ly, Moor - land winds out yon - - -

- - - - - - - - der.

The Two Sisters

INTRODUCTION

I wanted one of the stories in this book to take place in Kisimul Castle, which has belonged to the MacNeil clan since the twelfth century A.D. (or the fourteenth century, depending on which historian you believe.) *Kisimul* is from the Old Norse for "castle island," and the castle sits on a small rocky island off the south coast of the Isle of Barra, protected from raiders by the sea. Only the clan chief's "Keeper of the Keys" can take visitors inside, after a brief ride in his motorboat. John Allen MacNeil held that responsibility when I visited, and he gave me a wonderful tour that included stories, facts, and quiet moments to reflect on the lives of my ancestors who once roamed the halls. Robert Lister MacNeil, forty-fifth chief, began the restoration of Kisimul Castle in 1937, and it is now a powerful reminder of the legends of Vikings, landlords, battles, and the sea.

"Two Sisters" is a ghost story, one that I have told for many years. It is based on an English ballad. So what is it doing in a collection of tales from the faery world of the Hebrides Islands?

When I visited Barra, I was repeatedly told the story of a haunted house on the island. It concerns three drowned sailors who were buried on the Isle of Barra. A house was built on top of their graves, and their spirits now wander through the rooms. "You can hear the rubbing of the oil-skins that they wear," someone whispered to me at the hotel, and, "No one has been able to live there because of the ghosts." Although the islanders denied believing in the faery folk, the stories of the haunted house were passed on to me very seriously, and when I casually suggested to friends that I might spend the night in the house, everyone shifted uneasily in their chairs and said, "Aye, you could try to do that. Hope we see you in the morning." (I did not try, and I shall always regret that.)

So I knew ghosts were a part of the lore of Barra, but I thought they were not part of faery lore. I was wrong. Both W. Y. Evans-Wentz, in *The Fairy Faith in Celtic Countries* and Katharine Briggs, in *An Encyclopedia of Fairies*, refer to the theory that some faeries are the spirits of the dead. The *sluagh,* or faery hosts, are particularly evil because they are the unfor-given dead. Evans-Wentz quoted Marian MacLean of Barra as saying, "The hosts used to go after the fall of night, and more particularly about midnight. You'd hear them going in fine weather against a wind like a covey of birds" (p. 108).

The ghost in "Two Sisters" is not one of the *sluagh,* but a spirit who seeks the truth of her death. It will be her sister, perhaps, who will roam the world at midnight, unforgiven.

The Two Sisters

An Da Phiuthar[1]

There lived a lady by the North Sea shore
Lay the bent to the bonnie broom
Two daughters were the babes she bore.
Fa la la la la la la la la la.
As one grew bright as in the sun
Lay the bent to the bonnie broom
So dark-haired grew the other one.
Fa la la la la la la la la la.

Two sisters they were but as different as the sea and the moor. One was small, with long golden hair and blue eyes that were alive with joy. She flirted and teased with everyone in her father's castle, from cook to piper. She was quick to laugh, and she loved to dance, wherever her tiny feet touched earth or stone.

Not so, the older sister. She was tall and slender, with long dark hair, and eyes the color of the mist. She preferred her own company, and she spent her days reading what few books could be found on the island. Her smiles were few, shared only with her sister, and she never danced.

As different as these two girls were, there was one thing they both enjoyed: *A' mhuir*,[2] the sea. Every day they would walk, arm in arm, to the rocky shore, sometimes to watch the ships return, sometimes just to enjoy the waves crashing below them as the salty breezes caressed their faces. As they stood at the edge of the sea, the wind would blow their hair behind them, and the long yellow and black locks would intertwine, like ebony laced with gold.

Then, one day, everything in their lives changed.

---

1. ahn da FYOO-er
2. ah voor

There came a knight to the castle door
Lay the bent to the bonnie broom
He'd traveled far to be their woo'er.
Fa la la la la la la la la la.
He courted one with gloves and rings
Lay the bent to the bonnie broom
But loved the other above all things.
Fa la la la la la la la la la.

It was the older sister who caught Sir William's eye at first. He was charmed by her darkness and mystery. Hoping to see one of her rare smiles, he brought her gifts: white silk gloves with pearl buttons, a ring of amethyst and amber, a lace pillow to lay her head upon when he could not be with her. He wrote her poems about her eyes, and he read to her from leather-bound books that she had never seen before. The dark-haired girl gave her heart to Sir William, and she laughed at how easy it was to love. More than once, she was seen dancing down the halls of the castle.

But one evening, as the two sisters and the knight sat together sharing a song about a sailor who went to sea and never returned, the older girl noticed how Sir William's eyes seemed to linger on the hands of the fair-haired girl as she played her harp. His hazel eyes, and the blue eyes of the younger sister, gazed long, too long, at each other. The next evening the two of them shared a memory of a walk they had taken on the moors that day, without the older sister. As the days and weeks went by, their discovery and joy of each other was seen by all, from cook to piper. The dark-haired girl watched and waited in cold silence, thinking how painful it was to love.

Late one night, the older girl sat alone in the bedroom she shared with her sister. She was remembering. And she was tearing the lace of the pillow Sir William had given her into small pieces, which fell into her lap. Suddenly, into the room burst the fair-haired girl, with a blush upon her cheeks and lips bruised by many kisses. She fell upon her knees in front of her sister and announced that she and Sir William were to be married in the spring. "I hope that you will be happy for us, dear sister," declared the younger girl. "And, of course, I want you to stand beside me at the wedding."

The dark-haired girl said nothing, only continued to tear the lace and gaze out the open window toward the sea. Finally, she nodded slightly, and as she stood and walked away, the pieces of lace fell to the floor, drifting and swirling about her feet in the wind. That night, as the two sisters lay side by side in their bed, a vine of cold hatred grew inside the belly of the one who had loved and lost. It twined its way tightly around her heart, and, in the morning it blossomed out of her mouth with these words:

"Oh, sister, sister, will you come with me"
Lay the bent to the bonnie broom
"To watch the ships sail out to sea?"
Fa la la la la la la la la la.
And as they stood on the windy shore
Lay the bent to the bonnie broom
The dark-haired girl pushed her sister o'er.
Fa la la la la la la la la la.
Sometimes she sank, sometimes she swam
Lay the bent to the bonnie broom
Crying, "Sister, give to me your hand!"
Fa la la la la la la la la la.
"Oh, sister, sister, let me live,"
Lay the bent to the bonnie broom.
"And all that's mine you'll surely have."
Fa la la la la la la la la la.
"It's your own true love I'll have and more."
Lay the bent to the bonnie broom.
"But you will never come to shore!"
Fa la la la la la la la la la.

The dark-haired girl stood upon the rocks, looking straight ahead. Never once did she look at her sister as the fair-haired girl was pulled down and washed away by the waves of the sea. When she was certain that the girl was gone, she turned and walked slowly back to the castle. She told a grief-stricken story about how her younger sister had slipped upon the wet stones and how she had tried to save her, but the girl had drowned. From cook to piper, everyone noticed that she never shed a tear, but they said it was because she cared too much.

Sir William stayed on at the castle, unable to leave the home where he had courted the girl he wished to marry. For weeks he grieved alone, walking the moors and the coast with no one at his side. But then one warm day he invited the dark-haired girl to accompany him. As they walked, he spoke only of the one who had died, and the sister listened in silence. For many days he talked of all the plans and dreams they had shared and how he did not think he could bear to live without her. And then one day he only mentioned his betrothed briefly and another day not at all. Time passed, and the two became inseparable, as they had once been, not so long ago.

One evening, as Sir William and the dark-haired girl sat by the fire, he asked her to be his wife. She did not speak her answer, but nodded slightly, all the while looking down at her hands, folded tightly in her lap.

The word spread quickly across the island that a wedding feast would soon be held at the castle. Musicians, storytellers, and poets came from far and wide to entertain the bride and groom and their guests. On the afternoon before the celebration was to begin, the performers gathered in the kitchen for their supper. One man, who had grown old playing the lyre, noticed a *clarsach,*[3] a harp, standing alone, close to the fire. "*Co' leis a' chlarsach sin?*[4] Whose harp is that?"

"*Is leamsa.*[5] 'Tis mine," answered a young man, standing tall and strong. "Why do you ask?"

"Because of the strings," he answered. "There are three that shimmer like gold. Is it because of the flames, or my tired eyes?"

"It is neither," answered the harpist. "Those three strings are as precious as gold, from the most beautiful woman I have ever seen."

"Now, that sounds like a story we all should hear!" The lyre-player pulled his stool closer. "Everyone gather 'round and listen to this tale well told."

"I'm afraid there's not much to tell," apologized the young man. "It happened several months ago, when I stopped at the miller's home to sing and play for my supper and bed. While I was there, a woman's body was washed up on the shore. Oh, what a bonnie lass she was, with long golden hair that wrapped its way about her throat and arms and tiny waist. I'd never seen anyone so lovely. Neither the miller's family nor I knew who she was, so we buried her here, beside the sea. But before we laid her in the coffin that I made, I took three strands of her hair, and that is what you see dancing in the light."

"And do they sing well, those *teudan orach,*[6] golden strings?"

"Well enough, though tonight will be the first time they have sung for anyone but me."

"Then we wish you luck, harpist. And we look forward to your song."

One by one, the performers entered the Great Hall to dance and sing and story tell for the guests. Finally, the only one left was the young harpist. He stepped quietly into the room, placed his *clarsach* upon a stone, and bowed to the Chief. "Accept my thanks, Lord, for inviting me here to help you celebrate this grand occasion, the marriage of your daughter to Sir William. I hope you will enjoy my song, as much as I have enjoyed bringing it to you."

---

3. KLAHR-sahkh
4. koh lesh ah KHLAHR-sahkh shin
5. SLYOOM-suh
6. CHEE-uh-dun OR-ahkh

The musician turned to his harp, but before he had a chance to raise his hands to the strings, the door to the Hall suddenly burst open and *gaoth fhuar*,[7] a cold wind, danced into the room. It twirled and rustled its way through the silk and velvet worn by the guests, then skipped across the stone floor to twine its way through the strings of the harp. The three golden strings began to shimmer and sparkle in the firelight, and the harpist stepped back in amazement, his hands clasped behind him.

> *And as the harp stood upon the stone,*
> *Lay the bent to the bonnie broom*
> *The strings began to sing alone.*
> *Fa la la la la la la la la la.*
> *The first string sang with a mournful sound,*
> *Oo-oo-oo-oo-oo-oo-oo-oo*
> *"I am the sister, the one who drowned."*
> *Oo-oo-oo-oo-oo-oo-oo-oo-oo-oo.*
> *The second string sang in words so free,*
> *Ee-ee-ee-ee-ee-ee-ee-ee*
> *"It was my sister who murdered me."*
> *Ee-ee-ee-ee-ee-ee-ee-ee-ee-ee.*
> *The third string sang, in words so low,*
> *Oh-oh-oh-oh-oh-oh-oh-oh*
> *"And surely now her tears will flow."*
> *Oh-oh-oh-oh-oh-oh-oh-oh-oh-oh.*

The tears did flow, from out of her misty eyes, down her cheeks, and into the hands that had pushed her sister to her death. The dark-haired girl was taken from the hall, and a month later she was hung from the gallows until dead. After she was buried, Sir William left the island and was never seen again.

The harp remained upon its stone in the Great Hall, untouched and silent of words. But sometimes, *gaoth fhuar*, the cold wind, would dance its way into the room, leap and skip across the floor, and twine between the strings so that the three golden hairs would play a sad and wordless tune for *an da phiuthar*, two sisters.

---

7. goo hoor

Songs

The Two Sisters

An Da Phiuthar

In this old Scottish ballad, the words "Lay the bent to the bonnie broom" refer to a form of protection against faeries. It was believed that if bent grass was laid on top of broom (brush), it would keep the faeries away from the home.

The words to this song were given to me somewhere by an audience member after a storytelling performance in Denver. She thought I should tell it and said, "The song goes on forever and ever, but I'm sure there's a good story in it." She was right, and I thank her, whoever she is.

There lived a lady by the North Sea shore.
Lay the bent to the bonnie broom
Two daughters were the babes she bore.
Fa la la la la la la la la la.
As one grew bright as in the sun
Lay the bent to the bonnie broom
So dark-haired grew the other one.
Fa la la la la la la la la la.
A knight came riding to the lady's door
Lay the bent to the bonnie broom
He'd traveled far to be their wooer.
Fa la la la la la la la la la.
He courted one with gloves and rings
Lay the bent to the bonnie broom
But loved the other above all things.
Fa la la la la la la la la la.

Oh, sister, will you go with me
Lay the bent to the bonnie broom
To watch the ships sail on the sea?
Fa la la la la la la la la la.
She took her sister by the hand
Lay the bent to the bonnie broom
And led her down to the North Sea strand
Fa la la la la la la la la la.
And as they stood on the windy shore
Lay the bent to the bonnie broom
The dark girl threw her sister o'er
Fa la la la la la la la la la.
Sometimes she sank, sometimes she swam
Lay the bent to the bonnie broom
Crying, "Sister reach to me your hand!"
Fa la la la la la la la la la.

---

1. ahn da FYOO-er

"Oh, sister, sister, let me live,"
Lay the bent to the bonnie broom
"And all that's mine I'll surely give."
Fa la la la la la la la la la.
"It's your own true love that I'll have and more,"
Lay the bent to the bonnie broom
"But thou shalt never come ashore."
Fa la la la la la la la la la.
And there she floated like a swan
Lay the bent to the bonnie broom
The salt sea bore her body on.
Fa la la la la la la la la la.
Two minstrels walked along the strand
Lay the bent to the bonnie broom
And saw the maiden float to land.
Fa la la la la la la la la la.
They made a harp of her breast bone
Lay the bent to the bonnie broom
Whose sound would melt a heart of stone
Fa la la la la la la la la la.
They took three locks of her yellow hair
Lay the bent to the bonnie broom

And with them strung the harp so rare.
Fa la la la la la la la la la.
They went into her father's hall
Lay the bent to the bonnie broom
To play the harp before them all.
Fa la la la la la la la la la.
But as they laid it on a stone
Lay the bent to the bonnie broom
The harp began to play alone.
Fa la la la la la la la la la.
The first string sang a doleful sound
Lay the bent to the bonnie broom
The bride her younger sister drowned.
Fa la la la la la la la la la.
The second string sang as they cried
Lay the bent to the bonnie broom
In terror sits the black-haired bride.
Fa la la la la la la la la la.
The third string sang beneath their bow
Lay the bent to the bonnie broom
And surely now her tears will flow.
Fa la la la la la la la la la.

The Sea Tangle *or* The Sisters

An Sgeir-Mhara[1]

This song tells of half-sisters, one overpowered by her jealousy. At low tide the two are lying together on a reef, close to the sea. The jealous one lulls the other to sleep by weaving the sea tangle into her hair and crooning a lullaby. The heat, the music, the lap of the waves, and the braiding of her hair send the other into a dream-like state. The jealous one leaves as the tide rises, and the last words of the drowning sister left behind are a croon to the babe she will never hold again.

> Tangle and hair, I weave ye,
> Fast to the rock I weave ye.
> Tangle and gold, I weave ye,
> Fast to the rock I weave ye.
> Far the haze upon the deep,
> On Kyle nor sea cool winds can breathe.
> Tangle and gold, tangle and gold,
> Gold unto gold, I weave ye,
> Fast to the rock I leave thee.
> By the shore, no pity wilt show, woman yonder?
> *Uvil, uvil, uvil, uvil,*[2]
> Jealous sister, here entic'd me,
> And hast left me here a-drowning.
> Cold my bed, cold and slimy,
> Wet wi' tears, wet wi' brine.
> Blessing of Jesus, blessing of mother,
> Blessing eternal be on my children.
> My little child, love of my cooing,
> Seek'st thou tonight thy mother's bosom,
> And if thou seek'st, vain is thy seeking,
> Full 'twill be of sea water.
> *Uvil! uvil! Uvil! uvil!*

---

1. ahn SKARE–VAR-ah; The Sea Tangle
2. OO-veel; the sister's cry of terror, similar to that of a wounded seabird.

The Two Sisters

There lived a la-dy by the North Sea shore. Lay the

bent to the bon-nie broom Two daugh-ters were the babes she bore.

Fa la la la la la la la la la

The Sea Tangle *or* The Sisters

Tan - gle and hair, I weave ye, Fast to the rock I weave ye. Tan - gle and gold, I weave ye Fast to the rock I weave ye, Far the haze up - on the deep, On Kyle nor sea cool winds can breathe. Tan - gle and gold Tan - gle and gold, Gold un - to gold, I weave ye, Fast to the rock I leave thee By the shore, no pi - ty wilt show, wo - man yon - der? U - vil, u -

chil - dren.

My litt - le child, love of my

coo - ing, Seek'st thou to - night thy mo - ther's bo - som,

And if thou seek' - st vain is thy seek - ing, Full 'twill

be of sea wa - ter. U - vil! U - vil!

U - vil! U - vil!

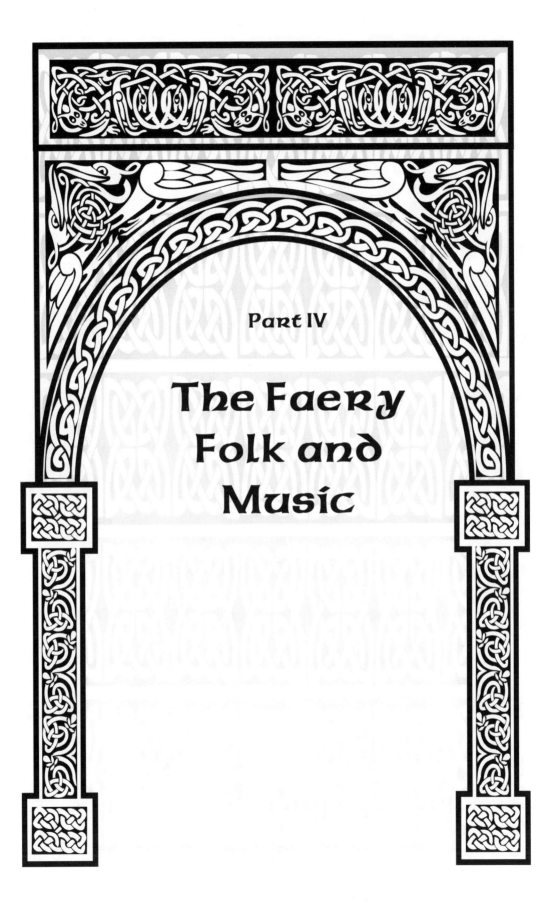

Part IV

The Faery Folk and Music

Christ Child's Lullaby *and* The Blind Woman and the Faeries

INTRODUCTION

The music of the Otherworld is a power that is both terrifying and wonderful. It can lead the mortal toward a world more beautiful than anything ever imagined on this earth, or it can possess the soul until there is nothing left but the body of what was once human. It can lead a man, woman, or child toward carefree dancing and play, or it can lead people to madness. The faery pipes or drums, whistles or singing, can give you a story to tell to your grandchildren, or it can make you leave your world behind and give up forever the chance to live with and love your family.

The theme of faeries and their music is one that occurs over and over again in the folktales of the Celtic world. One of the most valuable resources for finding these stories, and the music, is Kenneth Macleod's *The Road to the Isles: Poetry, Lore, and Tradition of the Hebrides.* Macleod spent his adult life collecting the music and lyrics of traditional Scottish songs. His massive publication, *Songs of the Hebrides*, written in conjunction with Marjory Kennedy-Fraser, is a priceless collection of piano and voice arrangements and the resource for most of the songs in this collection. But *The Road to the Isles* is the poetry and the story of those songs, as well as personal anecdotes and reflections about the people of the Hebrides.

The ideas for the next two stories, "The Christ Child's Lullaby," and "The Blind Woman and the Fairies," come from Macleod's book. The first is the story behind a poignant song sung by Mary Mother and passed on to mothers everywhere who lull their beloved children to sleep in their arms. The second is a simple tale of a woman whose power of hearing brings her the gift—or perhaps the curse—of being able to hear the faery folk. I have created my own versions of these tales because, as Macleod writes, "[O]ne has to weave the threads that are blown by the wind towards one: a half-remembered tale, a tag of a song, a proverb, a passing remark at a feast or in a sorrow" (p. 8).

Christ Child's Lullaby

Taladh Chriosta[1]

Who, among children, has not been foolish when they should have been wise? And who, among parents, has not been blind with anger when they should have been patient with love?

On the Isle of Uist, there was once a young lad who had lost his mother. His heart nearly died with her, for the boy was filled with longing for her gentle touch and lullabies. *"C'ait a' bheil mo mhathair?*[2] Where is my mother?" he would ask his father. "Is she happy or lonely?" His father could not answer his son's questions, but, in the hope of bringing joy back into their lives, he married again.

The boy could find no love for the stepmother in his already broken heart, so he gave her the pain of knowing his pain. When she would reach out to brush his cheek, he would turn his face away. When she tried to sing to him before he slept, he would pull the wool blanket over his head. And when she invited him to play with the half-sister that was soon born, the laddie left the house and went to sit beside his mother's grave. Each and every day he asked his father, *"C'aite bheil mo mhathair?* Where is my mother? Is she happy or lonely?"

Time passed, but the love between the boy and his stepmother did not come to be. As the lad grew, so did his sadness, for he found it easier to keep his heart broken rather than take the risk of mending it by loving again. The distance between stepson and stepmother became greater than either could forgive, and the woman no longer reached out for him or sang to him or even tried to understand him. When the boy was old enough to do his chores without a parent nearby, she sent him out of the house so that her anger at having her love refused would have a chance to rest from his anger at having his love lost. Nothing he did gave her pleasure or peace, and she spoke to him sharp and quick, with words like needles she hoped would stab at his heart, as his silence stabbed at hers.

---

1. TA-lugh KHREE-us-ta
2. katch uh vell moh VAH-her

And then, the father died, leaving behind three who were forced to live, but could not love, together.

The young lad became a young man, tall enough that he could look directly into his stepmother's eyes with the defiance of his age. He told her lies about where he was going and always returned late from wherever he'd been. He stole unimportant things from neighbors, and when his stepmother returned the wooden bowl or the knitted scarf she found hidden under his bed, the neighbors would say, "He is growing into the grave."

"No," she replied, "He is growing up to the gallows."

Finally, there was a day when neither could find the desire to say a kind word. "Outside with you!" she demanded, when he refused to help her with all that needed to be done. "Bring the cattle home this evening, milk them, and milk them well. Will you at least do that for the memory of your father, if not for me?"

The boy left, slamming the door so that the half-sister cried for an hour with fear.

At the end of the day the boy returned, later than expected, and the bucket of milk that he dropped at his stepmother's feet was only half full.

For a long while she stared at the bucket in silence, her hands balled into fists at her sides and her heart beating so loudly it seemed to fill the room. Finally, she looked up at him and said through clenched teeth, "I thought I told you to milk them well. Go back and do what I told you to do."

Before he would allow himself to consider the pain of his words, the boy hissed, "You are not my mother to tell me anything. I hate you!" He turned his back on her and walked away. Before she would allow herself to consider the pain of her words, she shouted back, "Son of another! There will be no luck on this house till you leave, but whoever heard of a luckless chick leaving of its own will?"

For a moment the boy stood still, and the room was loud with angry silence. Then, out the door he went, and by the time the moon rose, he was on the other side of the mountain.

That night, the stepmother could get neither sleep nor comfort. As she lay in her bed, all she could hear in her head were the terrible words he had spoken, but worse were the words she heard in her heart, the unforgivable words from her own mouth. Finally she arose and stepped out into a night that was filled with moon and sorrow. Without even realizing where it was that she was going, her bare feet walked across the sharpness of gorse and the roughness of stone, until she found herself on the other side of the mountain. It was there she stopped both movement and breath.

A Woman was sitting on a grassy knoll, and by the moon's light, the stepmother could see that in the Woman's arms lay a child, swaddled all in white. The Woman looked down at him, her face filled with only love, while she sang to him a lullaby.

> *My love, my dear, my darling thou,*
> *My treasure new, my gladness thou,*
> *My comely beauteous babe-son thou,*
> *Unworthy I to tend to thee.*

At the Woman's feet was the young lad, his face filled with a longing such as the stepmother had never seen.

> *O dear the eye that softly looks,*
> *O dear the heart that fondly love,*
> *Tho' but a tender babe thou art,*
> *The graces all grow up with thee.*

It was the sweetest music ever heard upon this earth, and the stepmother knew that the Woman who sang it was someone as rare and beautiful as the lullaby.

> *Hosanna to the Son of David,*
> *My King, my Lord, and my Savior!*
> *Great my joy to be song-lulling thee.*
> *Blessed among the women I.*

"God of the Graces!" whispered the stepmother. "It is Mary Mother. And she is doing what I ought to be doing, loving my son, whatever the pain." She fell to her knees, and wept the endless tears of a mother.

> *The fair white sun of hope Thou art,*
> *Putting the darkness into exile,*
> *Bringing mankind from a state of woe,*
> *To knowledge, light and holiness.*

Even after the singing ended, the stepmother remained kneeling in the heather, with her head bowed and her hands tightly clasped around those of her stepson. She did not remember how she and the boy came to be so close and so intertwined. When at last she looked up, no one was there in the moonlight, except for herself and the lad, asleep at her side. For the rest of the night, as the moon drifted away, she sang to him.

My love, my dear, my darling thou,
My treasure new, my gladness thou,
My comely beauteous babe-son thou,
Unworthy I to tend to thee.

And that is how "Christ Child's Lullaby" was first heard in the Isles.

Songs

Christic Child's Lullaby

Taladh Chriosta[1]

This is perhaps the only well-known song in this book. The words are from Father Allan MacDonald, king-priest of Eriskay, and the melody is said to have been "a Northern Sailor's folksong heard by Chopin in the Mediterranean." Mrs. John Macinnes of Eriskay sang the air for Marjory Kennedy-Fraser. I am including the Gaelic with this one because of the familiarity of the tune. For anyone who "has the Gaelic," the beauty of this lullaby is the same beauty heard when the sea lulls you to sleep under a canopy of stars and moon.

> My love, my dear, my darling thou,
> *Mo ghaol, mo ghradh, is m'eudail thu,*
> My treasure new, my gladness thou,
> *M'iunntas ur is m' eibhneas thu,*
> My comely beauteous babe-son thou,
> *Mo mhacan alainn ceutach thu,*
> Unworthy I to tend to thee.
> *Cha'n fhiu mi fhein bhi'd dhail.*
> I the nurse of the King of Greatness!
> *Tha mi 'g altrum Righ na Morachd!*
> I the mother of the God of Glory!
> *'S mise mathair Dhe na Glorach!*
> Am not I the glad to-be-envied one!
> *Nach buidhe, nach sona dhomhsa!*
> O my heart is full of rapture.
> *Tha mo chridhe lan de sholas.*
> O dear the eye that softly looks,
> *Mo ghaol an t-suil a sheallas tla,*

---

1. TA-lugh KHREE-us-ta

O dear the heart that fondly loves,
 Mo ghaol an cridh' tha liont' le gradh,
Tho' but a tender babe thou art,
 Ged is leanabh thu gun chail
The graces all grow up with thee.
 Is lionmhor buaidh tha ort a' fas.
Art King of Kings, art Saint of Saints,
 'S tu Righ nan Righ, 's tu Naomh nan Naomh,
God the Son of eternal age,
 Dia am Mac thu 's siorruidh t' aois,
Art my God and my gentle babe,
 'S tu mo Dhia 's mo leanabh caomh,
Art the King-chief of humankind.
 'S tu ard Cheann-feadhna chinne-daonda.
The fair white sun of hope Thou art,
 'S tusa grian gheal an dochais
Putting the darkness into exile,
 Chuireas dorchadas air fogairt,
Bringing mankind from a state of woe,
 Bheir thu clann-daoin' bho staid bhronaich
To knowledge, light and holiness.
 Gu naomhachd, soilleireachd, is eolas.
Hosanna to the Son of David,
 Hosanna do Mhac Dhaibhidh,
My King, my Lord, and my Saviour!
 Mo Righ, mo Thighearna, 's mo Shlan'ear!
Great my joy to be song-lulling thee.
 'S mor mo sholas bhi 'gad thaladh,
Blessed among the women I.
 'S beannaichte measg nam mnai mi.

Christ Child's Lullaby

My joy, my love, my dar - ling thou! My

trea - sure new, my rap - ture thou! My come - ly beau - tous

babe - son thou, Un - wor - thy I to tend to thee.

Ha - - le - - lu - i - a Ha - le - -

lu - i - a Ha - - le - - lu - i - a

Ha - le - lu - i - a

The Blind Woman and the Faeries

Am Boireannach Dall agus na Sithichean[1]

(*Note:* A *quern* was two flat, circular stones used for grinding. The upper stone had a handle inserted into a hole, and the grain was ground between the two stones. A waterfall may form natural querns by grinding away at the stones in the *linne*,[2] or pool, below.)

> *Second sight comes from the blood, second hearing from the blindness.*
>
> Gaelic saying

Each evening, on the Isle of Uist, a blind woman went out with the lads from town to bring the cattle home for milking. The woman had been blind since the day she was born, so she had never known the blue and silver of the sea, but she knew the ocean by its voice, both gentle and wild. She could not imagine the infinite colors of green on the moors, but she knew the moors by the smells of earth and flowers and rain. She did not know the faces of her neighbors, but she could identify each of the islanders by the quickness of their step or the rhythm of their breath.

She had the ears to hear, and the boys had the eyes to see. Together, the lads and the blind woman crossed the glens and climbed the rocks and searched the bogs for the cattle and calves that needed to be guided home. If truth be told, it was the woman who usually found the wayward cows, but she neither cared about nor expected to hear the truth from boys eager to prove their importance. She was content to be only part of the story.

But one day the story changed and became hers and hers alone.

---

1. ahm BUH-ren-ach dowl AH-goos nah SHEE-ack-an
2. lin

It was the blind woman who heard the lowing of a lost cow, but it was far away and the woman was weary from pulling heavy, wet skirts through the heather. So she told the boys the direction they should travel, and they willingly left her behind, eager to run at their own speed.

As the woman rested beside the pool, her world became a quilt of gentle sounds that wrapped around her and lulled her into sleep. The splash of the water-fall, the distant call of the cuckoo, the breeze that danced through her hair, the waves that endlessly caressed the rocky shores—the woman heard them all, and she let herself drift away, drift away, drift away.

> *Ho ro, hi ri, ri ri,*
> *Little roe-deer,*
> *Hear'st thou the linne a-querning?*

Someone was singing. The blind woman listened, drifting back to the world of the *linne* and voices sweeter than any other sound she knew.

> *Ho ro, hi ri, ri ri,*
> *Little need'st fear pulse of grinding,*
> *Music of querning in the linne,*
> *Ho ro, hi ri, ri ri,*
> *As it laughs and leaps and frolics.*
> *Ho ro, hi ri, ri ri.*

And then there was conversation about mushrooms and amethyst jewels and a mischief-maker named Whuppity Stoorie. About a hedgehog who was prickly in temperament as well as hide and a game of climbing spider webs. About the Nimble Men who fight their everlasting battle in the sky, leaving behind a field of dancing, colored lights. About the importance of golden hair for spinning and a place called *Tir nan Og*[3] and a knight named Tam Lin. The woman listened, under-standing enough of the words to know that those who were speaking were of the faery world. She almost laughed aloud when the two voices argued about who made the best heather ale, because the reasons given for the merits of one's brew over the other's were the same she had heard debated in the village between mortal men. She heard fear in the voices when they spoke of rowan and iron, and she felt fear in her own heart when they mentioned *Cat Sith*,[4] the Highland faery cat who was well-known for being as large as a dog.

---

3. cheer na nawg
4. kat shee

When the faeries were not talking or laughing, they were singing. Over and over, soft and loud, between each sentence and each thought, they sang the same song:

> *Ho ro, hi ri, ri ri,*
> *Little roe-deer,*
> *Hear'st thou the linne a-querning?*
> *Ho ro, hi ri, ri ri,*
> *Little need'st fear pulse of grinding,*
> *Music of querning in the linne,*
> *Ho ro, hi ri, ri ri,*
> *As it laughs and leaps and frolics.*
> *Ho ro, hi ri, ri ri.*

As the darkness of a new moon night began to erase the lines of stone and grass, the boys returned with the wayward cow. They found the blind woman asleep, her body curled around in a search for warmth. They woke her, and she walked home with them in silence.

But the next day, the woman was anything but silent. From the moment she awoke she began singing:

> *Ho ro, hi ri, ri ri,*
> *Little roe-deer,*
> *Hear'st thou the linne a-querning?*

All day long and into the night she sang the same tune and the same words, over and over. In the days that followed, she sang wherever she went and to whomever she was with. When the islanders asked her where she had learned this song, she would tell the story of sleeping by the *linne* and hearing the voices of faeries speaking of strange and wonderful things. She described them to whoever would listen, ending her tale by singing the song, then starting all over again. At first, the people would listen to her story and song, and they, too, were enchanted by what the woman remembered. But as days and weeks went by, they grew annoyed with hearing the same words and tune. People avoided her, tired of her endless chatter. The woman was no longer welcome to accompany the lads as they searched for the cattle, for she could not be silent long enough to listen.

Other women warned her of her foolishness. "Do you not know that it is forbidden to sing what the faeries sing and to tell what the faeries tell? Be silent, woman, or the black sorrow will come to you."

But the woman never seemed to realize that her story and song had been heard a thousand times. On and on she chattered, as if she truly could not stop.

Ho ro, hi ri, ri ri,
Little need's fear pulse of grinding.
Music of querning in the linne,
Ho ro hi ri, ri ri.
As it laughs and leaps and frolics.
Ho ro, hi ri, ri ri,
Ho ro, hi ri, ri ri,
Ho ro, hi ri, ri ri,
Ho ro, hi ri, ri ri. . . .

One evening, when it was to be a new moon night again, the blind woman went out with the lads in spite of their reluctance to have her company. When they reached the *linne,* she said she would wait for them by the waterfall, and they ran off, eager to escape her endless prattle about creatures they had no time to believe in. When the boys returned she was not there, neither did she return to the village on her own. The township women said, "Tonight there will be three singing

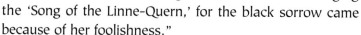

the 'Song of the Linne-Quern,' for the black sorrow came because of her foolishness."

The blind woman was gone and was never seen on this earth again. And who is to say whether it was indeed the black sorrow, or perhaps white joy, that came to her and took her to sing in the world of the faery folk, forever.

Songs

The Song of the Linne-Quern

Fuaim na Brathain anns an Linnidh[1]

This song was recorded from the singing of Catriona Campbell, a native of South Uist.

> Ho-ho ho-ro ho-ro
> Ho-ho ho-ro ho-ro
> Ho-ho-ro.
> Little roe-deer,
> Hear'st thou the linne a-querning?
> Ho hi ri-ri ho-ro
> Ho-ho ho-ro ho-ro
> Ho-ho-ro
> Ho-ho-ro.
> Little need fear pulse of grinding
> Music of querning in the linne
> Ho-ho ho-ro ho leo
> As it laughs and leaps and frolics
> Ho-ho ho-ro ho-ro

---

1. FOO-ahm nah BRA-hayn awns ahn LEAN-ee

The Song of the Linne-Quern

Ho - ho ho - ro ho - ro Ho - ho ho - ro ho - ro

Ho - ho - ro. Lit - tle roe-deer, Hearst thou the linn a - quer-ning?

Ho hi ri - ri ho-ro Ho - ho ho - ro ho-ro Ho - ho-ro

Ho - ho-ro. Lit - tle need fear pulse of grinding

Mu - sic of quern - ing in the linne Ho - ho ho - ro ho leo

As it laughs and leaps and fro-lics Ho - ho ho - ro ho - ro.

Finlay and the Faery Cowl

INTRODUCTION

Alasdair Alpin MacGregor wrote in *The Haunted Isles, or, Life in the Hebrides*, "I know of the existence, in staff notation, of fragments of faery music taken down in the Western Isles by those who actually heard them" (p. 79). He also wrote of a hollow on Mingulay from which one cannot see the ocean: "Hence the belief in olden times that this spot was the haunt of evil spirits; and even today this hollow is regarded by the natives of the Barra Isles as a place of ill-omen" (p. 79). His book was published in 1933; today it is not so easy to find those who believe in the existence of the Otherworld. When I was on Barra I was told, "Stories of faeries were just stories told to children." Yet for me the magic was still there, and anything was possible. Similarly, my parents visited Ireland in 1996, and my mother said, "I always felt that if I just turned around a bit faster, I would see one of the faery folk. But I was never quick enough."

That is how it is in the Hebrides and other parts of the Celtic world. The mist on the moors and the fog over the seas, unexplained appearances and disappearances, a history of "wee folk" driven underground, and druids who listened to trees—all have combined with the Celtic gift of imagination and exaggeration to create an unsurpassed ability to tell a tale.

This next story is from MacGregor's *The Haunted Isles*. I chose it because I was intrigued by the fact that both human and faery offer a love that is unforgiving, cruel, and selfish. Neither the Otherworld, nor our world, is always as it seems.

Finlay and the Faery Cowl

Fhionnladh agus na Curracd Sith[1]

Evil spirits haunted the well, the people of Mingulay said. Its waters were crystal clear, but its depths were bottomless, they said. Even the cattle avoided the well, and so did the Islefolks.

They said more. There was a prophecy about the well, and those with the second sight foretold that a beautiful maiden would be strangled in a battle between man and beast and faery.

"Who will win, man or beast?" the children asked the *sgeulaiche*,[2] but the storyteller had no answer.

And then Finlay, son of Iain, was born. He grew to be a handsome man, and he had a sweetheart, the fairest of all the maidens on Mingulay. She loved him with each breath of her gentle mouth and each beat of her innocent heart. But Finlay let the seasons pass without asking her to be his bride.

"A foolish lad," the Islefolks said. But the maiden waited, believing in the goodness of the promises he made.

One day, while searching for sheep lost in the mist of the mountain *Beinn a' Phi*,[3] Finlay heard music.

"Who is it that sings so sweetly?" asked Finlay , but there was no answer. The tune seemed to come from the wind itself. "Come, show yourself," demanded Finlay. "Are you faery or human?"

" 'Tis faery I am," said a voice, and from out of the clouds stepped a woman more beautiful than any of Finlay's foolish dreams. Her cowl, a long hooded cloak, drifted and swirled, drifted and swirled. "And 'tis lonely I am, Finlay, son of Iain. Will you sit beside me, here in this hollow?"

---

1. HEWN-lag AH-gus nah KOOR-ack shee
2. SKEE-ah-likh-uh
3. bane ah fee

Finlay could no more have refused the faery woman than touch the moon. He sat beside her, and his eyes were so filled with the beauty of her that he never noticed the well, dark and unholy, close by them. She sang to him so that his head was filled with wonderful things such as only the faery folk know. And then, in one brief instant when he closed his eyes and sighed with longing, she was gone.

That night Finlay could not sleep but tossed and turned in his bed until he was covered with the sweat of fever and nightmare. As soon as the sun rose, he returned to the mountain, wandering and listening and hoping until, finally, he heard the wind-voice again.

"Is it you, come back to me?" asked Finlay into the wind.

"Aye, I have come back." And there she was, still wrapped in the cowl that was darker than a moonless night. " 'Tis cold I am, Finlay, son of Iain. Will you sit with me and hold my hands?"

So he sat with her, holding her hands and listening to the voice that wooed him away to thoughts of the Otherworld, and *Tir nan Og*,[4] and her. When he bowed his head to look down at her hands because he felt only cold bone and no warm flesh, she slipped away.

Finlay moaned in his bed all night, for his heart was no longer his own. He gave no thought to his sweetheart, who lay in her own bed not so very far away and cried, for her heart was lost as well.

The next morning Finlay went back to the hollow on *Beinn a' Phi*, and he called for his faery love. She came to him, her beautiful shape seeming to form out of the rock and heather. " 'Tis cold I am, Finlay, son of Iain," she said. "Will you sit with me and wrap your arms around me?" So of course he did, next to the unhallowed well, and she gifted to him the Faery Cowl that fell from her forehead to the earth. She wrapped it around Finlay, and Finlay wrapped his arms around her, so that the two became one, and his shape was no longer his own.

From out of the black and bottomless depths of the well stepped *an t-each-uisge*,[5] the water horse. "*Do bhas os do chionn, Fhionnladh mhic dhaoine!*[6]—Death upon thy head, O Finlay, son of man!" The beast screamed and bared its teeth, and its eyes were blood-red. Finlay realized that his arms were empty, but the faery cowl held him to the earth, so that he could not move.

---

4. cheer na nawg; Land of the Ever Young
5. ahn chekh OOSH-guh
6. do vas aws do KEY-on HEWN-lag vic GOON-yeh

It was Finlay's sweetheart, milking her cows, who heard his screams. She did not think of the prophecy as she ran to the summit. She did not wonder about the maiden who would be strangled, or of the story the *sgeulaiche* could not finish. All she thought of as she ran was Finlay, and Finlay, and Finlay, and Finlay.

They say that the well is haunted now by more than evil spirits, for it was the sweetheart of Finlay who was strangled, and foolish, luckless Finlay who was dragged by a beast into the never-ending darkness.

Songs

Faery's Love Song

Tha Mi Sgith[1]

Why should I sit and sigh,
Pu-in' bracken, pu-in' bracken,
Why should I sit and sigh,
On the hill-side dreary?
When I see the plover rising
Or the curlew wheeling,
Then I trow my mortal lover
Back to me is stealing.
Why should I sit and sigh,
Pu-in' bracken, pu-in' bracken,
Why should I sit and sigh
All alone and weary?
When the day wears away,
Sad I look a-down the valley.

Ilka sound wi' a stound
Sets my heart a-thrilling.
Why should I sit and sigh,
Pu-in' bracken, pu-in' bracken,
Why should I sit and sigh
All alone and weary?
Ah! but there is something wanting,
Oh! but I am weary.
Come, my blythe and bonnie lad,
Come over the knowe to cheer me.
Why should I sit and sigh,
Pu-in' bracken, pu-in' bracken,
Why should I sit and sigh,
Parted frae my dearie?

---

1. hah me ski

Faery's Love Song

Why should I sit and sigh, Pu - in' brack - en pu - in' brack - en, Why should I sit and sigh, On the hill - side drea - ry? When I see the plov - er ris - ing Or the cur - lew wheel - ing, Then I trow my mor - tal lov - er Back to me is steal - ing. Why should I sit and sigh Pu - in' brack - en pu - in' brack - en Why should I sit and sigh All a - lone and wea - ry? When the day wears a - way, Sad I look a - down the val - ley. Il - ka sound wi' a stound Sets my heart a - thrill - ing. Why should I sit and sigh, Pu - in' brack - en

pu - in' brack - en. Why should I sit and sigh, All a - lone and

wea - ry? Ah! but there is some - thing want - ing, Oh! but I am

wea - ry. Come, my blythe and bon - nie lad, come over the knowe to

cheer me. Why should I sit and sigh, Pu - in' brack - en

pu - in' brack - en, Why should I sit and sigh, Part - ed frae my

dear - - - - - - - ie?

WE CAN TEACH YOU TO HEAR THESE THINGS...

©nancy chien-eriksen '01

The Piper's Cave

INTRODUCTION

While I was on Barra I had the good fortune to meet Roddy Nicholson and his brother-in-law, Jimmy Campbell. They showed me ancient standing stones in cow pastures, taught me how to rake cockles, and took me to the cemetery to visit the graves of priests and more Mac-Neils than I care to remember. This is what I wrote about Roddy and Jimmy in my journal:

> *Roddy is big and burly, generous to a fault, always offering me a Coke or crisps (potato chips), and buying drinks for everyone at the Craigard. He's never been married, and when he's not with the merchant marines, he lives in a renovated house with his mother, relying on others to get him around the island because he cannot drive. Roddy loves the sea and the fishing boat he brought from Ireland above all things. He's always dressed in a blue boiler suit and handmade green fisherman's cap. He's been patient with trying to teach me the Gaelic, and I've given him the name "Ten Minutes," for that is his reply whenever I ask a question of time or distance. "No problem, Heather. Ten minutes, and we'll be there."*

Jimmy is visiting from Oban. He is opinionated and outspoken and has a clever wit that keeps me laughing when we gather with the fishermen in the late afternoon for a "wee dram." He has given me a nickname that has more meaning for me than he realizes. It comes from the fact that I have quickly become recognizable as I walk around the island with my turquoise backpack, stuffed with snacks, camera, and cassette tape player. I am also known for usually being late whenever I agree to meet friends because I lose track of time while I'm listening to stories. So Jimmy combined the two characteristics, and one afternoon when I walked into the Craigard an hour later than promised, Jimmy called out, "Oh, look! Here comes the Pack O' Lies!" It is a perfect name for a storyteller.

I do enjoy listening to them with their friends, switching from the Gaelic to English, talking the usual talk of life on the island, especially as it relates to weather.

"It's a good day."

"Aye. (long pause) Should be better on Wednesday."

"Aye. (long pause) It was terrible last Thursday."

"Och, well, that's the way it is then. Not bad today, though."

"The wind was terrible last year. Blew the roof off my house."

"Your house?"

"Aye."

"The one you just fixed up?"

"Aye."

"Oh, you've got a wonderful view there."

"A wonderful view doesn't do you much good when you haven't got a roof."

One afternoon Roddy took me out on his boat to see the seals. Although we didn't see too many, I had a wonderful time visiting with fishermen who were clipping the claws of crabs. I also got my first chance at steering a boat. As we traveled around the southeast coast, Roddy pointed out "The Piper's Cave" and told me the legend of how it got its name. Later, I found the story briefly mentioned in "Barra: A Step by Step Guide," a pamphlet published by the Clan Macneil Association of America in 1987. It is a tale that is told in many parts of Scotland, sometimes referring to fiddlers, sometimes pipers. Whenever I tell this story, I make sure I have a piper to accompany me. The last words and the echo of the pipes mingle to create a haunting ending.

The songs of the sea and of the bagpipes are in the heart of every Scottish islander. If you add to that a curious interest in the possibility of the faery world, you have all the ingredients to create a story of magic and music.

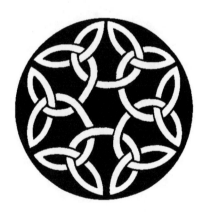

The Piper's Cave

Uamh a' Phiobaire[1]

The music of Iain the piper was well-known from the pebbled shores of Vatersay to the windswept moors of Uist. People said Iain must have been born with a chanter in his hands and a bag under his arm, for no one could remember a time when he wasn't playing his *piob-mhor*,[2] bagpipes. He piped calls to battle for the chief and his fighting men in Kisimul Castle and reels for the crofters' *ceilidhean*[3] on the islands. Fishermen heard Iain's airs as they loaded their nets onto boats in the morning and as they mended their nets on shore in the evening. No marriage was celebrated and no death was mourned without the music of Iain's bagpipes.

"The pipes are the breath of my soul," Iain said to his family and friends. "I couldna' wake up in the morning if I was not sure the pipes would be there for me to play." And play he did, charming and enchanting his listeners, young and old, male and female.

But it wasn't just the human folk who enjoyed his lively jigs or mournful *ceol mhor*.[4] Birds perched on nearby branches, heads cocked and wings tucked, occasionally chirping along with the tune. Sheep and cows chewed and watched with unending patience, and rabbits would hop and dance in the moonlight, oblivious to the owls that waited for the protective spell to end. Most faithful of all was Iain's little black terrier, Dobhran,[5] named for his otter-quickness and playfulness. The dog was always at Iain's side, and because the music was Iain's life it had become part of Dobhran's life as well.

---

1. OO-uv ah FEE-bah-ruh
2. peeb vor
3. KAY-lee-un; gatherings
4. kyohl vor; bagpipe music
5. DOH-run

Now, even though Iain was known as the best piper in all of the Islands, he was never satisfied with his own skills and knowledge. Iain was always eager to perfect his fingering technique or to learn a new tune. "*Abair fuaim!*"[6] he would say when he was unhappy with his playing. "What a noise!" And then he would start the tune all over again. "I know it could be played better."

"Iain," said his friend, Malcolm the Fisherman, "who could possibly play any better than you?"

"Why, the faeries, of course," Iain replied, gazing out toward *Uamh an Oir*,[7] the Cave of Gold. For it was there, along the rocky coast of Barra, that people said they often heard the music of the faery folk mingling with the music of the sea. Iain was sure he had heard the haunting sound of bagpipes, and it sounded like nothing he was able to play. "They play the wind," said Iain, "and the waves. I have heard the faery bagpipes and I will never be content until my pipes sound like theirs."

One moonlit night the people of Barra gathered for a *ceilidh*[8] at the seaside cottage of Malcolm and his wife. Stories were told, songs were sung, dances were danced, and more than enough *uisge-beatha*,[9] the water of life, known as whiskey, was shared. Iain played better than anyone had ever heard before. It was as if his fingers could not stop and seemed to send flashes of light out into the darkness. As the final note of his last tune drifted out across the moors his listeners wept for the beauty of it. "Och, Iain," Malcolm said. "The faeries themselves must be envious tonight." Iain said nothing, but looked toward *Uamh an Oir*.

When the evening ended, Iain began his journey back home, Dobhran trotting along at his heels. Iain walked in silence, which was not like him; his steps were usually accompanied by the trill of his pipes. Finally, Iain spoke to the terrier. "Do you think it's true, Dobhran? Do you think the faeries have heard me play and are envious of my music?"

"Aye, that we are." Iain jumped nearly out of his skin, thinking that his dog had answered him. He stared down at Dobhran, whose teeth were bared and whose fur bristled.

"It was not your dog that spoke," said a gentle voice. "It was myself." There, standing in the heather, was a young woman, not much taller than the terrier. The moon was behind her so that Iain could not see her face, only her long hair that blew about her like a cape of darkness and light. The skin of her hands and feet shone with their whiteness, but her eyes remained a secret.

---

6. AH-ber FOO-um
7. OO-uv un or
8. KAY-lee
9. OOSH-kuh BAY-huh

The terrier growled. "Hush," said Iain as he placed his hand on the dog's head, but Dobhran remained stiff and uneasy.

"Who are you?" Iain asked the strange woman, although he was quite sure he knew the answer.

"I am what you call a faery, of course, although we do not call ourselves by that word. We are simply *An Teaghlach*."[10]

"The Family?"

"Yes. *An Teaghlach a' Cheo*,[11] The Family of the Mist."

"And you have heard my music?"

"Aye, that we have. It is quite wonderful, Iain, so wonderful that I have come to ask you to teach us."

"That cannot be possible! It is your music that has been my dream."

"What you played tonight was the fulfillment of that dream. We can, however, teach you about listening."

"But I do listen."

"To what?"

"To the wind. And the ocean. To the birds and to the river and to children laughing."

"Have you heard the cry of a star falling? Have you heard the song a spider sings as she spins her web, or how a starfish calls to the sea when it has been cast out on the shore? You've heard the laughter of children, but have you heard an otter laugh? Have you heard the lullaby of the mist, Iain? We can teach you to hear these things, and you can teach us to play the music. Will you come with me, and learn to hear, and play, *ceol an t-saoghail*,[12] the music of the world?"

"Will I be able to return to my world when I am ready?"

"I promise you this, Iain the Piper. If you come to us willingly and without greed, you may return to your world whenever you wish. All you need to do is ask."

"Then I will come."

"That's fine, then. Wait for the dark of the moon, Iain, and listen for the music of *Uamh an Oir*." With that said, the faery was gone, disappearing into the mist over the moor.

Iain told his friends nothing about his magical encounter that night, for he was afraid it had only been his own wishful thinking combined with *uisge-beatha* that created the faery. But when fourteen days had passed, Iain went to Malcolm's home and told him where he would be going that night.

---

10. an CHUH-lahkh; family
11. ahn CHUH-lahkh ah khyoh
12. kyohl ahn TOO-ul

"Are you daft, Iain?" asked Malcolm. "You'll never be coming back!"

"I will be coming back. As soon as I've learned about listening to *ceol an t-saoghail*, the music of the world. Think of it, Malcolm. I'll be learning more than I had ever hoped for, from those who know more than any mortal ever could. Will you take me, in your boat, to *Uamh an Oir*, tonight?"

"Is there nothing I can say that would make you change your mind?"

"And give up hearing the lullaby of the mist? No, my friend, there is nothing you can say."

So it was that Iain the Piper, Dobhran the terrier, and Malcolm the Fisherman went together in a wee boat that dark night to *Uamh an Oir*. Iain held a lantern for Malcolm to steer by, and when they were as close to the shore as the fisherman dared to be, the two men wrapped the lantern and the bagpipes in oilskin. Then they swam to shore, holding the bundle over their heads while the dog paddled close by his master, as always.

When they reached land Malcolm lit the lamp. "Are you sure, Iain, that this is what you want to be doing? Can you not be satisfied with your music as your friends are?"

Iain sat listening to the sea as it was sucked in, and then spat out, by the cave. "How could I ever be satisfied if I could never play the song of a falling star? Och, Malcolm, think of all that I am going to see and hear! And I will be back, as soon as I have heard *ceol an t-saoghail*." Iain stood and called to his dog. "Will you come with me, Dobhran? Will you live with me and the faery folk?"

Dobhran looked up at Iain, and when his master walked toward the cave, the dog, as always, followed along beside him. But when he got to the entrance the terrier stopped and growled, every hair bristling with fear and his eyes a startling white in the darkness. He trembled, and then, as Iain blew the pipes to life, the dog answered the call of the music he had always known and followed Iain the Piper into the cave.

Malcolm stood upon the shore, listening to the music of the pipes as it echoed and faded into the world below. He knew, as well as he knew his own name, that he would never see Iain again. And not because the faeries held the piper against his will in the Otherworld, but because of what Iain had said to Malcolm earlier that night. "Think of all that I am going to see and hear! And I will be back, as soon as I have heard *ceol an t-saoghail*, the music of the world." It would be Iain's choice to stay with the faery folk, forever.

The people of the Isle of Barra say that, sometimes, if you listen carefully to the music of the sea at *Uamh an Oir* you will also hear the music of *piob-mhor*, bagpipes. Someone's dog once answered a playful bark he heard inside the cave by running through the entrance and into the darkness. The dog soon returned, alone and trembling, without a single hair left on him.

That's what they say. That's the story they tell of what has come to be known as *Uamh a' Phiobaire*, The Piper's Cave.

Songs

The Sea-Longing

An Ionndrainn-Mhara[1]

This song was collected from Anne Monk of Benbecula. As Marjory Kennedy-Fraser explains, "And if one is ever haunted by the restless movement of the wind and sea in the isles, it is in the songs themselves that there is no escape from it" (Kennedy-Fraser and Macleod, *Songs of the Hebrides*, p. xxvii).

> Sore sea-longing in my heart,
> Blue deep Barra waves are calling,
> Sore sea-longing in my heart.
> Glides the sun, but ah! how slowly,
> Far away to luring seas!
> Sore sea-longing in my heart,
> Blue deep Barra waves are calling,
> Sore sea-longing in my heart.
> Hear'st, O sun, the roll of waters,
> Breaking, calling by yon Isle?
> Sore sea-longing in my heart,
> Blue deep Barra waves are calling,
> Sore sea-longing in my heart.
> Sun on high, ere falls the gloamin'
> Heart to heart thou'lt greet yon waves.
> Mary Mother, how I yearn,
> Blue deep Barra waves are calling,
> Mary Mother, how I yearn.

---

1. ahn EWE-uhn-dry-uhn–VAR-ah

The Sea-Longing

Sore sea - long - ing in my heart, Blue deep Bar - ra waves are calling sore sea - long - ing in my heart. Glides the sun, but ah! how slow - ly, Far a - way to lur - ing seas! Sore sea - long - ing in my heart, Blue deep Bar - ra waves are call - ing sore sea - long - ing in my heart. Hear'st O sun, the roll of wa - ters, Break - ing, call - ing by yon Isle? Sore sea - long - ing in my heart, Blue deep Bar - ra waves are call - ing, sore sea - long - ing

in　　my　　heart.　　Sun　　on　　high,　　ere　　falls　　the　　gloam - in',

Heart　　to　　heart　　thou'lt　　greet　　yon　　waves.　　Ma - ry　　Mo - ther,

how　　I　　yearn,　　Blue　　deep　　Bar - ra　　waves　　are　　call - ing,

Ma - ry　　Mo - ther,　　how　　I　　yearn.

Appendix: Protection from the Faery Folk

If you believe in the magic, you must also believe in the power of that magic. The power can be used for fun and trickery, or evil and treachery. So it is wise to have your own power, the power of protection. Following are some words and objects believed to provide protection from the faery folk.

Christian Symbols: The Bible, the Cross, a Prayer

Particularly effective was the Lord's Prayer, spoken aloud. Mothers protected their babies from faeries by hanging open scissors over the cradle to make a cross of cold iron. Other powerful materials were rowan wood, coral, and amber. Crossing one's own body, a cross scratched on the ground, or the crossing of two roads were all effective protection against faeries. When marked on the top of cakes, a cross prevented faeries from dancing on them.

Churchyard Mold and Holy Water
These could be carried or strewn.

Bread and Salt
Both were regarded as sacred symbols, one of life and the other of eternity.

Iron
A nail in the pocket or a knife in a doorway would protect a mortal from faery power.

Bells
Especially effective were church bells and iron bells worn round the necks of sheep and oxen.

Turning Clothes
Clothes worn inside-out would change the wearer's identity.

Four-Leafed Clover
This was the strongest of the plants and herbs that acted as countercharms, breaking faery glamor.

St. John's Wort
The herb of Midsummer, this was potent against not only faeries but also evil spirits and the Devil.

Daisies
Little field daisies, worn as a chain around the neck, kept children safe from being kidnapped by the faery folk.

Red Verbena
Perhaps because of its pure and brilliant color, this was considered almost as potent as St. John's Wort.

Rowan Wood
No home should be without! A staff, a cross, and a bunch of the tree's ripe berries were all protection from faery powers. **Ash** was a good substitute, if rowan was not available.

Moving Water
One could leap to safety across running water, especially a southward-flowing stream. But beware of kelpies!

Horseshoes
Horseshoes hung above the house and stable doors, they protected humans and livestock because they were made of iron.

Self-Bored Stones
These were stones with holes bored through by water. If you looked through the hole, you could see faeries. Hung over stalls, they were effective in brushing off faeries, who were fond of riding horses around the fields at night until the animals were exhausted.

Milk
Dairy maids would place a quantity of milk on a hollow stone so the *gruagach*, a form of brownie, would not beat them with a rod.

Cats
According to *Strange Old Scots Customs and Superstitions*, "On many Scots farms, when a calf was born, a cat was set on its neck, drawn along its back, and then seated on the cow's back. Next it was drawn down one side of the mother and pulled up the other, tail foremost." This was done to protect cows from *trows*, a type of spirit that would fire a stone arrow and wound the cow or carry the cow away when it was in a weakened state.

Primroses
When eaten, primroses make the invisible visible, so one can see faeries. According to Brian Froud and Alan Lee in *Faeries*, "If one touches a faerie rock with the correct number of primroses in a posy, the way is opened to faerie land and faerie gifts, but the wrong number opens the door to doom" (p. 138).

Flax on the Floor; a Twig of Broom; a Sock Under the Bed; a Pig's Head Drawn on the Door; a Twig of Oak, Ash, and Thorn Bound Together with Red Thread.
With so many protections against faeries, one wonders how they ever manage to perform their trickery. But mortals being what they are (forgetful, unbelieving, careless, self-assured), the faery folk have plenty of chances to do what they do best: be more clever than the human folk.

REFERENCES

Briggs, Katharine. *An Encyclopedia of Fairies: Hobgoblins, Brownies, Bogies, and Other Super-natural Creatures*. New York: Pantheon Books, 1976.

Froud, Brian, and Alan Lee. *Faeries*. New York: Harry N. Abrams, 1978.

"Strange Old Scots Customs and Superstitions." Adapted from *Old Scottish Customs—Local and General* by E. J. Guthrie. Glasgow, Scotland: Lang Syne Publishers, 1989.

 # Glossary

It is not often that you will meet someone in the United States who "has the Gaelic." It is a difficult language, and the speaking of it is not at all like the spelling of it. I greatly appreciate the patient assistance of George Seto and Liam Cassidy, members of GAIDHLIG-B, a Gaelic listserv. In addition, Glenn Wrightson, a Gaelic instructor in Colorado, graciously met with me over coffee and spoke into a tape recorder, so I could incorporate some of his translations into my storytelling. Frank Dagostino from the CELTIC-L listserv generously provided me with the Welsh that was needed.

A' chuthag (ah KHOO-uk): The cuckoo

A' mhaighdeann-mhara (ahm MY-tchen-VAR-ah): Maiden of the sea; mermaid

A' Maighdeann-Mhara 'Us Fear-Ron (ahm MY-tchen-VAR-ah oos FER-rohn): The Mermaid and the Selkie

A' mhuir (ah voor): The sea

Abair fuaim! (AH-ber FOO-um): What a noise!

Am Beicear a Bagh a' Chaisteal (ahm BAY-ker ah bahg ah KHASH-chul): The Baker of Castlebay

Am Beicear agus an Sithichean (ahm BAY-ker att-goosahn SHEE-ack-an): The Baker and the Faeries

Am Boireannach Dall agus na Sithichean (ahm BUH-ren-ach dowl AH-goos nah SHEE-ack-an): The Blind Woman and the Faeries

Am Bron Mara (ahm brawn MAH-rah): The Sea Sorrow

An Cadal Trom (ahn CAT-al trum): The Profound Sleep

An Da Phiuthar (ahn da FYOO-er): The Two Sisters

An da shealladh (ahn dah HYAHL-uh): The second sight

An Ionndrainn-Mhara (ahn EWE-uhn-dry-uhn-VAR-ah): The Sea-Longing

An Laoidh Diarmaid (ahn LOO-ee JEE-arm-itch): The Lay of Diarmaid

An Sgeir-Mhara (ahn SKARE-VAR-ah): The Sea Tangle

An t-each-uisge (ahn chekh OOSH-guh): The water horse

An t-each-uisge agus an Nighean (ahn chekh OOSH-guh AH-gus ahn NEE-un): The Kelpie and the Girl (literal translation: The Water Horse and the Girl)

An t-Eilean Dorcha (ahn-CHAY-lun DOR-uh-khuh): The Dark Island

An Teaghlach (ahn CHUH-lahkh): The Family

An Teaghlach a' Cheo (ahn CHUH-lahkh ah khyoh): The Family of the Mist

Ann am Barraigh (OW-n ahm BARE-eye): Prettiest girl in Barra

Aran nan Sithichean (AIR-ahn nu SHEE-ack-an): Bread of the Faeries

Bairn (bayrn): Baby

Bi samhach! (bee SAH-vahkh): Be quiet!

Caidealan Cuide Rium Fhin Thu (CATCH-el-an COOTCH-uh REE-com heen ooo): Uist Cradle Croon

C'ait a' bheil mo mhathair (katch uh vell moh VAH-her): Where is my mother?

Cat Sith (kat shee): Highland faery cat

Ceilidh (KAY-lee): Gathering

Ceilidhean (KAY-lee-un): Gatherings

Ceol (kyohl): Music

Ceol an t-saoghail (kyohl ahn TOO-ul): Music of the world

Ceol mhor (kyohl vor): Classical music of the bagpipes

Ceud mile failte (keed MEE-luh FAHL-chuh): A hundred thousand welcomes

Chaol Ile (kyle EES-lah): Isle of Isla

Chaol Mhuile (kyle MOO-lah): Isle of Mull

Chi sinn na chi sinn (khee sheen nah khee sheen): We shall see what we shall see

Chuilein a ruin (ah hool-IN ah roon): Child love, don't wake 'til morn

Claddedigaith y Lleuad (klah-theh-DEE-geith uh HLEI-ahd): The Buried Moon (Welsh)

Clarsach (KLAHR-sahkh): Harp

Co' leis a' chlarsach sin? (koh lesh ah KHLAHR-sahkh shin): Whose harp is that?

Croit (krohch): Farm or croft

Cronan na Eich-mhara (KROW-nahn nah ACHE-VAH-rah): The Skye Water Kelpie's Lullaby

Cronan na Maighdinn-Mhara (KROW-nan nah MY-cheen–VAR-ah): The Mermaid's Croon

Currachd sith (KUR-ack shee): Faery cowl

Daoine sidhe (DOON-yeh shee): Faery folk

Dhiarr a' Mhuir a Bhith ga Tadhal (yeer ah vorr ah vee gah tahl): The Sea Claims Her Own

Dobhran (DOH-run): Otter

Draoidheachd (DROO-ee-ahkh): Magic

Falamh (FAH-lav): Empty

Fhionnladh agus na Curracd Sith (HEWN-lag AH-goos nah KOOR-ack shee): Finlay and the Faery Cowl

Flath na Finne (flah nah fin): Chief of the Finne

Flath nam Fear (flah nam fer): Chief of men

Fuaim na Brathain anns an Linnidh (FOO-ahm nah BRA-hayn awns ahn LEAN-ee): The Song of the Linne-Quern

Gaoth fhuar (goo hoor): Cold wind

Geasa (GEES-ah): A spell or charm

Geo (joe): A bay with high cliffs on either side

Gradh-an donn (GRAH-yun doun): Loved one brown

Gruagach (GROO-ugh-ahkh): Maiden

Gruagach-Mhara (GROO-ugh-ahkh–VAR-ah): Seal-Maiden (literal translation: sea maiden)

Gu brath (goo brah): Forever

Gwragedd Annwn (GWRA-geth a-NOON): Water faeries (Welsh)

Gwraig Annwn (gwrag a-NOON): Lady of the Lake (Welsh)

Is leamsa (SLYOOM-suh): It is mine

Iasgair (EE-us-ger): Fisherman

Latha math dhuibh (lah mah GOO-iv): Good day to you

Latha math dhuibh fhein (lah mah GOO-iv hayn): Good day to you (reply)

Leanamh tacharan (LYEN-uv TAKH-uh-run): Changeling child

Linne (lin): The pool beneath a waterfall

Mara (MAH-rah): Sea

Meddygon Myddfai (meth-UH-gone MUHTH-vie): Physicians of Myddfai

Mo sgian dubh (mo SKEE-an doo): My black (or dark) knife

Niall Noighiallach (NE-yu NUY-yee-uhl-ach): Niall of the Nine Hostages

Null a Mhonadh e Nall a Mhonadh (nool ah VOHN-uh eh naul ah VOHN-uh): Wind on the moor (literal translation: Hither and thither across the moor)

Oisean na Fheinne (AWE-shen nah heen): Oisean of the Finne

Oran Macneill na Barraigh (ORE-an MACH-neel nah BARE-eye): Ballad of Macneill of Barra

Piob-mhor (peeb vor): Bagpipes

Righ nan Sithichean (ree nun SHEE-ack-an): King of the Fairies

Ruidhle (RYEE-uh-luh): Reel

Samhain (SOUW-in): End of Summer celebration occurring on November 1

Sannt (sount): Greed

Seanachas na Maighdinn-Mhara (SHEN-ack-as nah MY-cheen–VAR-ah): Legend of the Mermaid

Seanamhair (SHEN-uh-ver): Grandmother

Sgeir dubh (skare doo): Black rock

Sgeulachdan (SKEE-lahk-un): Stories

Sgeulaiche (SKEE-ah-likh-uh): Storyteller

Sios (SHEE-us): Down

Sithean (SHEE-hun): Faery knoll

Sithichean (SHEE-ack-an): Faeries

Sluagh (SLOO-ah): Spirits of the dead; faery hosts

Taladh Chriosta (TA-lugh KHREE-us-ta): Chist Child's Lullaby

Tapadh leibh (TAH-puh lev): Thank you

Teudan orach (CHEE-uh-dun OR-ahkh): Golden strings

Tha Mi Sgith (hah me ski): Fairy's Love Song

Thoir an aire (HOH-er un EHR-uh): Be careful

Tir na Mhiann na Chridhe (cheer nah VEE-awn nah KREE-yuh): Land of Heart's Desire

Tir nan Og (cheer na nawg): Land of the Ever Young

Tuatha De Danann (TOO-ah jay DAH-nuhn): The people of the goddess of Dana or Danu

Uamh a' Phiobaire (OO-uv ah FEE-bah-ruh): The Piper's Cave

Uamh an Oir (OO-uv un or): Cave of Gold

Uisge-beatha (OOSH-kuh BAY-huh): Water of life; whiskey

 **Bibliography**

CELTIC FOLKLORE AND MYTHOLOGY

Arrowsmith, Nancy, and George Moorse. *A Field Guide to the Little People*. New York: Hill & Wang, 1977.

Bang, Molly. *The Buried Moon and Other Stories*. New York: Scribner, 1977.

Briggs, Katharine. *Abbey Lubbers, Banshees & Boggarts: An Illustrated Encyclopedia of Fairies*. New York: Pantheon Books, 1979.

——. *A Dictionary of British Folk-Tales in the English Language*. Bloomington: Indiana: University Press, 1971.

——. *An Encyclopedia of Fairies: Hobgoblins, Brownies, Bogies, and Other Supernatural Creatures*. New York: Pantheon Books, 1976.

——. *The Personnel of Fairyland*. Detroit: Singing Tree Press, 1971.

——. *The Vanishing People: Fairy Lore and Legends*. New York: Pantheon Books, 1978.

Campbell, J. F. *More West Highland Tales*. Edinburgh, Scotland: Birlinn, 1994.

——. *Popular Tales of the West Highlands*. Edinburgh, Scotland: Birlinn, 1994.

——. *Popular Tales of the West Highlands, Volume 2*. Edinburgh, Scotland: Birlinn, 1994.

Chant, Joy. *The High Kings: Arthur's Celtic Ancestors*. New York: Bantam Books, 1983.

Chapman, Jean. *Haunts and Taunts: A Book for Hallowe'en and All the Nights of the Year*. Chicago: Children's Press International, 1983.

Chmelova, Elena. *Celtic Tales*. New York: Exeter Books, 1982.

Colum, Padraic, ed. *A Treasury of Irish Folklore*. New York: Bonanza Books, 1983.

Douglas, Ronald Macdonald. *Scottish Lore and Folklore*. New York: Beekman House, 1982.

Ellis, Peter Berresford. *A Dictionary of Celtic Mythology*. New York: Oxford University Press, 1992.

Evans-Wentz, W. Y. *The Fairy-Faith in Celtic Countries*. New York: Carol Publishing, 1990.

Finlay, Winifred. *Folk Tales from Moor and Mountain*. New York: Roy Publishers, 1969.

——. *Tales from the Hebrides and Highlands*. London: Kaye & Ward, 1978.

Froud, Brian, and Alan Lee. *Faeries*. New York: Harry N. Abrams, 1978.

Green, Miranda. *Celtic Goddesses: Warriors, Virgins and Mothers*. New York: George Braziller, 1996.

Gregory, Lady Isabella. *Gods and Fighting Men*. Gerrards Cross, England: Colin Smythe, 1979.

Hodges, Margaret. *Buried Moon*. Boston: Little, Brown, 1990.

——. *Hauntings: Ghosts and Ghouls from Around the World*. Boston: Little, Brown, 1991.

Jacobs, Joseph. *Celtic Fairy Tales*. New York: Dover, 1968.

——. *English Fairy Tales*. 3rd ed. New York: G. P. Putnam's Sons, 1898.

——. *More English Fairy Tales*. New York: G. P. Putnam's Sons, 1910.

Kennedy-Fraser, Marjory, and Kenneth Macleod. *Songs of the Hebrides*. New York: Boosey, 1921.

Leach, MacEdward. *The Ballad Book*. New York: A. S. Barnes, 1955.

——. *The Book of Ballads*. New York: Heritage Press, 1967.

Lehane, Brendan. *The Enchanted World: Legends of Valor*. Alexandria, VA: Time-Life Books, 1984.

Lochhead, Marion. *The Other Country: Legends and Fairy Tales of Scotland*. London: Hamish Hamilton, 1978.

Mackinnon, Nan. *Tales, Songs, and Tradition from Barra and Vatersay*. Castlebay, Isle of Barra: Barra and Vatersay Local History Society, n.d.

Macleod, Kenneth. *The Road to the Isles: Poetry, Lore, and Tradition of the Hebrides*. Edinburgh, Scotland: Robert Grant & Son, 1927.

Manning-Sanders, Ruth. *A Book of Charms and Changelings*. New York: E. P. Dutton, 1972.

——. *A Book of Mermaids*. New York: E. P. Dutton, 1968.

Mayo, Margaret. *The Book of Magical Horses*. New York: Hastings House, 1977.

McGarry, Mary. *Great Folk Tales of Old Ireland*. New York: Bell Publishing, 1972.

McHargue, Georgess. *The Impossible People: A History Natural and Unnatural of Beings Terrible and Wonderful*. New York: Holt, Rinehart & Winston, 1972.

McKee, Christian M. *Scottish Folklore, Legend and Superstition*. Baltimore: Gateway Press, 1983.

McNeill, F. Marian. *The Silver Bough: Scottish Folk-Lore and Folk-Belief, Volume One*. Edinburgh, Scotland: Canongate Publishing, 1989.

Minard, Rosemary. *Womenfolk and Fairy Tales*. Boston: Houghton Mifflin, 1975.

Moray, Ann. *A Fair Stream of Silver*. London: Longmans, Green, 1965.

Morrison, Norman. *Hebridean Lore and Romance*. Inverness, Scotland: Highland News, 1936.

Nic Leodhas, Sorche. *Heather and Broom: Tales of the Scottish Highlands*. New York: Holt, Rinehart & Winston, 1960.

Nichols, Ross. *The Book of Druidry*. London: Aquarian Press, 1990.

——. *Sea-Spell and Moor-Magic: Tales of the Western Isles*. New York: Holt, Rinehart & Winston, 1968.

——. *Thistle and Thyme*. New York: Holt, Rinehart & Winston, 1962.

Osborne, Mary Pope. *Mermaid Tales from Around the World*. New York: Scholastic, 1993.

Pugh, Ellen. *More Tales from the Welsh Hills*. New York: Dodd, Mead, 1971.

Rhys, John. *Celtic Folklore: Welsh and Manx*. New York: Arno Press, 1980.

Robertson, Ronald Macdonald. *Selected Highland Folk Tales*. England: Newton Abbott, 1977.

Sheppard-Jones, Elisabeth. *Scottish Legendary Tales*. Edinburgh, Scotland: Thomas Nelson & Sons, 1962.

Sikes, Wirt. *British Goblins: Welsh Folk-Lore, Fairy Mythology, Legends and Traditions*. Yorkshire, England: EP Publishing, 1973.

Suits, Michael. "A Visit to Tara." *The Galley* (Fall/Winter 1995).

Time-Life Books. *The Enchanted World: Fabled Lands*. Alexandria, VA: Time-Life Books, 1986.

——. *The Enchanted World: Fairies and Elves*. Chicago: Time-Life Books, 1984.

——. *The Enchanted World: Ghosts*. Chicago: Time-Life Books, 1984.

Williamson, Duncan. *Tales of the Seal People: Scottish Folk Tales*. Brooklyn, NY: Interlink Books, 1992.

Wilson, Barbara Ker. *Scottish Folk-Tales and Legends*. New York: Henry Z. Walck, 1963.

Web Sites

Celtic Folklore. © January 2001 P.J. Brown. Available: http://www.belinus.co.uk/folklore/Homeextra.htm. (Accessed May 10, 2001).

Faery Lore. Available: http://www.treeleaves.com/folklore/faery.html. (Accessed May 10, 2001).

THE HEBRIDES OF SCOTLAND

Boswell, James. *Boswell's Journal of a Tour to the Hebrides with Samuel Johnson, LLD*. New York: Literary Guild, 1936.

Bray, Elizabeth. *Discovery of the Hebrides: Voyages to the Western Isles, 1745–1883*. Edinburgh, Scotland: Birlinn, 1996.

Cooper, Derek. *Hebridean Connection: A View of the Highlands and Islands*. London: Fontana, 1991.

——. *The Road to Mingulay: A View of the Western Isles*. London: Routledge & Kegan Paul, 1985.

Johnson, Alison. *Islands in the Sound: Wildlife in the Hebrides*. London: Victor Gollancz, 1989.

Kennedy-Fraser, Marjory, and Kenneth Macleod. *School Songs from the Hebrides*. Glasgow: Paterson's Publications, n.d.

————. *Songs of the Hebrides*. New York: Boosey, 1921.

MacDonald, Fiona. *Island Voices*. Edinburgh, Scotland: Canongate Press, 1994.

MacGregor, Alasdair Alpin. *The Haunted Isles, or, Life in the Hebrides*. London: Alexander Maclehose, 1933.

Macneil, Robert Lister. *Castle in the Sea*. London: Collins, 1964.

MacPherson, John. *Tales from Barra: Told by the Coddy*. Edinburgh, Scotland: Birlinn, 1992.

McPhee, John. *The Crofter and the Laird*. New York: Farrar, Straus & Giroux, 1969.

Shaw, Margaret Fay. *From the Alleghenies to the Hebrides*. Edinburgh, Scotland: Canongate Press, 1993.

"Strange Old Scots Customs and Superstitions." Adapted from *Old Scottish Customs—Local and General* by E. J. Guthrie. Glasgow, Scotland: Lang Syne Publishers, 1989.

Web Sites

Castles of the World. © 1995–2001. Available: http://www.castles.org/Chatelaine/KISIMUL. (Accessed March 7, 2001).

Electric Scotland. Available: http://www.electricscotland.com. (Accessed May 10, 2001).

Hebrides.com. © 2001. Available: http://www.hebrides.com. (Accessed March 7, 2001).

The Internet Guide to Scotland: Isle of Barra. © 1996–2001. Available: http://www.scotland-inverness.co.uk/barra.htm. (Accessed: March 7, 2001).

Scottish Culture. © 2001 About.com, Inc. (Accessed May 10, 2001).

THE MACNEIL CLAN

Byrne, Francis John. *Irish Kings and High-Kings*. London: B. T. Batsford, 1973.

Clan Macneil Association of America. *Barra: A Guide to the Island Commemorating the Reacquisition of Kisimul in 1937 and the Gathering of Clan Neil, July 23–26, 1987*. Charlotte, NC: Clan Macneil Association of America, 1987.

Ellis, Peter Berresford. *A Dictionary of Celtic Mythology*. New York: Oxford University Press, 1992.

——. *A Dictionary of Irish Mythology*. Santa Barbara: ABC-CLIO, 1987.

Logan, James. *The Clans of the Scottish Highlands: The Costumes of the Clans*. New York: Alfred A. Knopf, 1980.

Macneil, Ian Roderick. *Kisimul Castle, Isle of Barra, Scotland*. Stornoway: Stornoway Gazette, 1974.

Macneil, Robert Lister. *Castle in the Sea*. London: Collins, 1964.

——. *The Clan Macneil*. Bruceton Mills, WV: Scot Press, 1985.

Macneil-Sanders, ed. *The Galley: A Publication of the Clan Macneil Association of America*. Pasadena, CA.

Moncreiffe, Sir Iain. *The Highland Clans: The Dynastic Origins, Chiefs and Background of the Clans and of Some Other Families Connected with Highland History*. New York: Bramhall House, 1967.

Munro, R. W. *Kinsmen and Clansmen*. London: Johnston & Bacon, 1971.

Roy, James Charles. *The Road Wet, the Wind Close: Celtic Ireland*. Dublin: Gill & Macmillan, 1986.

Web Sites

The Clan MacNeil Association of America. © 1995–2000. Available: http://www.macneilgroup.com/neilclan.htm. (Accessed May 10, 2001).

Isle of Barra, Eilean Bharraigh. Available: http://www.isleofbarra.com. (Accessed May 10, 2001).

The McNeill Family Genealogy. © Roy McNeill 1999. Available: http://home.pacbell.net/roymc/Index.htm. (Accessed May 10, 2001).

THE ANCIENT CELTS

Bellingham, David. *Celtic Mythology*. Secaucus, NJ: Chartwell Books, 1990.

Gerhard, Herm. *The Celts: The People Who Came Out of the Darkness*. New York: Barnes & Noble Books, 1975.

James, Simon. *The World of the Celts*. London: Thames & Hudson, 1993.

Time-Life Books. *Celts: Europe's People of Iron*. Alexandria, VA: Time-Life Books, 1994.

Wood, Juliette. *The Celts: Life, Myth, and Art*. New York: Stewart, Tabori & Chang, 1998.

Web Sites

Celtic Heart. Available: http://celt.net/Celtic. (Accessed March 7, 2001).

Celtic History. Available: http://phys.canterbury.ac.nz/ ~ physdpm/celtic .html. (Accessed May 10, 2001).

Celt.Net: An Online Community. © 1998. Available: http://www.celt.net. (Accessed March 7, 2001).

Elementary Course of Gaelic. Available: http://www.smo.uhi.ac.uk/gaidhlig /ionnsachadh/ECG. (Accessed May 10, 2001).

Every Celtic Thing on the Web: Angus Og's Hotlinks to the Celts. Available: http://og-man.net. (Accessed March 7, 2001).

Gaelic Learners: Gaelic for Beginners Course. © Dalriada Celtic Heritage Trust. Available: http://www.dalriada.co.uk/html/gaelic_learners.html. (Accessed May 10, 2001).

Rivendell Educational Archive: Celtic History. © 1996–2001 Leigh Denault. Available: http://www.watson.org/rivendell/historycelt.html. (Accessed May 10, 2001).

Recommended Reading

The Changeling Child

For more stories about changelings, I recommend reading:

Briggs, K. M. "The Fairies and the Smith." In *The Personnel of Fairyland*. Detroit: Singing Tree Press, 1971.

Finlay, Winifred. "The Fishwife and the Changeling." In *Folk Tales from Moor and Mountain*. New York: Roy Publishers, 1969.

Manning-Sanders, Ruth. *Charms and Changelings*. New York: E. P. Dutton, 1972.

Nic Leodhas, Sorche. "The Stolen Bairn and the Sidh." In *Womenfolk and Fairy Tales* edited by Rosemary Minard. Boston: Houghton Mifflin, 1975.

For information about changelings, I recommend reading:

Briggs, Katharine. *Abbey Lubbers, Banshees & Boggarts: An Illustrated Encyclopedia of Fairies*. New York: Pantheon Books, 1979.

———. *An Encyclopedia of Fairies: Hobgoblins, Brownies, Bogies, and Other Supernatural Creatures*. New York: Pantheon Books, 1976.

McHargue, Georgess. "The Faery Folk." In *The Impossible People: A History Natural and Unnatural of Beings Terrible and Wonderful*. New York: Holt, Rinehart & Winston, 1972.

Time-Life Books. *The Enchanted World: Fairies and Elves*. Chicago: Time-Life Books, 1984.

The Baker and the Faeries

For more stories about humans and faeries, I recommend reading:

Briggs, K. M. "King Herla." In *Abbey Lubbers, Banshees & Boggarts: An Illustrated Encyclopedia of Fairies*. New York: Pantheon Books, 1979.

———. "The Return of Oisin." In *The Personnel of Fairyland*. Detriot: Singing Tree Press, 1971.

———. "True Thomas." In *The Personnel of Fairyland*. Detroit: Singing Tree Press, 1971.

Finlay, Winifred. "Jamie and the Silky of Black Heddon." In *Folk Tales from Moor and Mountain*. New York: Roy Publishers, 1969.

———. "Tamlane." In *Folk Tales from Moor and Mountain*. New York: Roy Publishers, 1969.

Lochhead, Marion. "Thomas the Rhymer," "Whuppity Stourie," "The Queen of Elfland's Nurse," and "King Orfeo and His Queen." In *The Other Country: Legends and Fairy Tales of Scotland*. London: Hamish Hamilton, 1978.

McHargue, Georgess. "The Faery People." In *The Impossible People: A History Natural and Unnatural of Beings Terrible and Wonderful.* New York: Holt, Rinehart & Winston, 1972.

Nic Leodhas, Sorche. "The Woman Who Flummoxed the Fairies." In *Heather and Broom: Tales of the Scottish Highlands.* New York: Holt, Rinehart & Winston, 1960.

Time-Life Books. "Thomas the Rhymer" and "A Benison from the Blessed Court." In *The Enchanted World: Fairies and Elves.* Chicago: Time-Life Books, 1984.

Wilson, Barbara Ker. "The Faery and the Kettle." In *Scottish Folk-tales and Legends.* New York: Henry Z. Walck, 1963.

Faery Bread

Macgregor, Alasdair Alpin. *The Haunted Isles, or, Life in the Hebrides.* London: Alexander Maclehouse, 1933.

Niall of the Nine Hostages

To learn more about Niall of the Nine Hostages and the High Kings, read:

Byrne, Francis John. *Irish Kings and High-Kings.* London: B. T. Batsford, 1973.

Chant, Joy. *The High Kings: Arthur's Celtic Ancestors.* New York: Bantam Books, 1983.

Ellis, Peter Berresford. *A Dictionary of Celtic Mythology.* New York: Oxford University Press, 1992.

———. *A Dictionary of Irish Mythology.* Santa Barbara: ABC-CLIO, 1987.

Green, Miranda. *Celtic Goddesses: Warriors, Virgins and Mothers.* New York: George Braziller, 1996.

Mac Call, Seamus. *And So Began the Irish Nation.* New York: Longmans, Green, 1931.

Matthews, Caitlin. "Niall of the Nine Hostages: An Excerpt from Encyclopaedia of Celtic Wisdom." *The Galley* (Spring/Summer 1996).

Newark, Tim. *Celtic Warriors, 400 B.C.–1600 A.D.* New York: Blandford Press, 1986.

Nichols, Ross. *The Book of Druidry.* London: Aquarian Press, 1990.

Roy, James Charles. *The Road Wet, the Wind Close: Celtic Ireland.* Dublin: Gill & Macmillan, 1986.

Stone, Hilliard. "Tales of the Macneils." *The Galley* (Spring/Summer 1998).

Suits, Michael. "A Visit to Tara." *The Galley* (Fall/Winter 1995).

Oisean of the Finne

For additional versions of the story of Oisean, Fionn, and the Finne, I recommend:

Briggs, Katharine. *An Encyclopedia of Fairies, Hobgoblins, Brownies, Bogies, and Other Supernatural Creatures.* New York: Pantheon Books, 1976.

Campbell, J. F. *Popular Tales of the West Highlands, Volume 2*. Edinburgh: Birlinn, 1994.

Colum, Padraic, ed. *A Treasury of Irish Folklore*. New York: Bonanza Books, 1983.

Evans-Wentz, W. Y. *The Fairy Faith in Celtic Countries*. New York: Carol Publishing, 1990.

Froud, Brian, and Alan Lee. *Faeries*. New York: Harry N. Abrams, 1978.

Gregory, Lady Isabella. *Gods and Fighting Men*. Gerrards Cross, England: Colin Smythe, 1979.

Lehane, Brendan. *The Enchanted World: Legends of Valor*. Alexandria, VA: Time-Life Books, 1984.

McGarry, Mary. *Great Folk Tales of Old Ireland*. New York: Bell, 1972.

Time-Life Books. *The Enchanted World: Fabled Lands*. Alexandria, VA: Time-Life Books, 1986.

The Kelpie and the Girl

For more stories about kelpies, I recommend reading:

Briggs, K. M. "The Water Horse and the Water Bull." In *The Personnel of Fairyland*. Detroit: Singing Tree Press, 1971.

Finlay, Winifred. "The Water-Horse of Barra." In *Folk Tales from Moor and Mountain*. New York: Roy Publishers, 1969.

Mayo, Margaret. "Sheena and the Water Horse." In *The Book of Magical Horses*. New York: Hastings House, 1977.

Nic Leodhas, Sorche. "The Bride Who Out Talked the Water Kelpie." In *Thistle and Thyme*. New York: Holt, Rinehart & Winston, 1962.

Sheppard-Jones, Elisabeth. "John Macdonald and the Kelpie." In *Scottish Legendary Tales*. Edinburgh: Thomas Nelson & Sons, 1962.

Wilson, Barbara Ker. "Morag and the Water Horse." In *Scottish Folk-Tales and Legends*. New York: Henry Z. Walck, 1963.

For information about kelpies, I recommend reading:

Briggs, Katharine. *An Encyclopedia of Fairies: Hobgoblins, Brownies, Bogies, and Other Supernatural Creatures*. New York: Pantheon Books, 1976.

Froud, Brian, and Alan Lee. *Faeries*. New York: Harry N. Abrams, 1978.

McKee, Christian M. *Scottish Folklore, Legend, and Superstition*. Baltimore: Gateway Press, 1983.

Time-Life Books. *The Enchanted World: Fairies and Elves*. Chicago: Time-Life Books, 1984.

The Mermaid and the Selkie

For more stories about mermaids, I recommend reading:

Osborne, Mary Pope. *Mermaid Tales from Around the World*. New York: Scholastic, 1993.

Robertson, Ronald Macdonald. *Selected Highland Folk Tales*. London: David and Charles, 1977.

For more stories about selkies, I recommend reading:

Briggs, K. M. "The Seal Fisher and the Roane." In *The Personnel of Fairyland*. Detroit: Singing Tree Press, 1971.

Nic Leodhas, Sorche. "The Daughter of the King Rong." In *Heather and Broom: Tales of the Scottish Highlands*. New York: Holt, Rinehart & Winston, 1960.

Robertson, Ronald Macdonald. *Selected Highland Folk Tales*. London: David and Charles, 1977.

Williamson, Duncan. *Tales of the Seal People: Scottish Folk Tales*. Brooklyn, NY: Interlink, 1992.

For information about mermaids and selkies, I recommend reading:

Arrowsmith, Nancy. *A Field Guide to the Little People*. Hill & Wang, 1977.

Briggs, Katharine. *Abbey Lubbers, Banshees & Boggarts: An Illustrated Encyclopedia of Fairies*. New York: Pantheon Books, 1979.

———. *A Dictionary of British Folk-Tales in the English Language*. Bloomington: Indiana University Press, 1971.

———. *An Encyclopedia of Fairies: Hobgoblins, Brownies, Bogies, and Other Supernatural Creatures*. New York: Pantheon Books, 1976.

McKee, Christian M. *Scottish Folklore, Legend and Superstition*. Baltimore: Gateway Press, 1983.

Thomson, David. *The People of the Sea*. Canongate Classics, 1954, 1996.

Legend of the Mermaid

For more stories about mermaids, I recommend reading:

Briggs, Katharine. *A Dictionary of British Folk-Tales in the English Language, Part B, Folk Legends, Volume I*. Bloomington: Indiana University Press, 1971.

Froud, Brian, and Alan Lee. "Lutey and the Mermaid." In *Faeries*. New York: Harry N. Abrams, 1978.

Kennedy-Fraser, Marjory, and Kenneth Macleod. *Songs of the Hebrides*. New York: Boosey, 1921.

Morrison, Norman. *Hebridean Lore and Romance*. Inverness, Scotland: Highland News, 1936.

Osborne, Mary Pope. *Mermaid Tales from Around the World*. New York: Scholastic, 1993.

Robertson, Ronald Macdonald. *Selected Highland Folk Tales*. London: Alexander Maclehose, 1977.

Lady of the Lake

For additional versions of "Lady of the Lake," I recommend:

Briggs, Katharine. "Gwragedd Annwn." In *An Encyclopedia of Fairies: Hobgoblins, Brownies, Bogies, and Other Supernatural Creatures*. New York: Pantheon Books, 1976.

Froud, Brian, and Alan Lee. "The Gwragedd Annwn." In *Faeries*. New York: Harry N. Abrams, 1978.

Jacobs, Joseph. "The Shepherd of Myddvai." In *Celtic Fairy Tales*. New York: Dover, 1968.

Manning-Sanders, Ruth. *A Book of Mermaids*. New York: E. P. Dutton, 1968.

Rhys, John. "Undine's Kymric Sisters." In *Celtic Folklore: Welsh and Manx*. New York: Arno Press, 1980.

Sikes, Wirt. "Chapter III." In *British Goblins: Welsh Folk-Lore, Fairy Mythology, Legends and Traditions*. Yorkshire, England: EP Publishing, 1973.

The Sea Claims Her Own

Kennedy-Fraser, Marjory, and Kenneth Macleod. *Songs of the Hebrides*. New York: Boosey, 1921.

Macleod, Kenneth. *The Road to the Isles: Poetry, Lore, and Tradition of the Hebrides*. Edinburgh: Robert Grant & Son, 1927.

The Buried Moon

For additional versions of "The Buried Moon," I recommend reading:

Bang, Molly. "The Buried Moon." In *The Buried Moon and Other Stories*. New York: Scribner, 1977.

Chapman, Jean. "The Dead Moon." In *Haunts and Taunts: A Book for Hallowe'en and All the Nights of the Year*. Chicago: Children's Press International, 1983.

Hodges, Margaret. *Buried Moon*. Boston: Little, Brown, 1990.

Jacobs, Joseph. "The Buried Moon." In *More English Fairy Tales*. New York: G. P. Putnam's Sons, 1910.

Pugh, Ellen. "The Buried Moon." In *More Tales from the Welsh Hills*. New York: Dodd, Mead, 1971.

The Two Sisters

For additional versions of "The Two Sisters," I recommend reading:

Briggs, Katharine. *An Encyclopedia of Fairies*. New York: Pantheon Books, 1976.

Evans-Wentz, W. Y. *The Fairy Faith in Celtic Countries*. New York: Carol Publishing, 1990.

Hodges, Margaret. "The Haunted Harp." In *Hauntings: Ghosts and Ghouls from Around the World*. Boston: Little, Brown, 1991.

Jacobs, Joseph. "Binnorie." In *English Fairy Tales*. 3rd ed. New York: G. P. Putnam's Sons, 1898.

Leach, MacEdward. "The Two Sisters." In *The Ballad Book*. New York: A. S. Barnes, 1955.

———. "The Two Sisters." In *The Book of Ballads*. New York: Heritage Press, 1967.

Silber, Irwin, and Fred Silber. *Folksinger's Wordbook*. New York: Oak Publications, 1973.

Time-Life Books. "Song of the Sorrowing Harp." In *The Enchanted World: Ghosts*. Alexandria, VA: Time-Life Books, 1984.

Christ Child's Lullaby *and* The Blind Woman and the Faeries

Kennedy-Fraser, Marjory, and Kenneth Macleod. *Songs of the Hebrides*. New York: Boosey, 1921.

Macleod, Kenneth. *The Road to the Isles: Poetry, Lore, and Tradition of the Hebrides*. Edinburgh: Robert Grant & Son, 1927.

Finlay and the Faery Cowl

MacGregor, Alasdair Alpin. *The Haunted Isles, or, Life in the Hebrides*. London: Alexander Maclehose, 1933.

The Piper's Cave

For more stories about pipers and faeries, I recommend reading:

Kennedy-Fraser, Marjory, and Kenneth Macleod. *Songs of the Hebrides*. New York: Boosey, 1921.

Robertson, Ronald Macdonald. "Lure of the Pipes." In *Selected Highland Folk Tales*. London: David and Charles, 1977.

Sheppard-Jones, Elisabeth. "The Piper of Sutherland." In *Scottish Legendary Tales*. Edinburgh: Thomas Nelson & Sons, 1962.

Wilson, Barbara Ker. "The Piper of Keil." In *Scottish Folk-Tales and Legends*. New York: Henry Z. Walck, 1963.

Index

✹ About the Author

Following the tradition of her grandfather, aunt, and mother, Heather is a storyteller who believes that stories are for all ages. Raised as an "army brat," she learned to enjoy traveling and experiencing different cultures and lifestyles. Heather planned to be an actress and received a degree in theater from the University of Missouri, Columbia. However, she soon realized that a love for stories was in her soul, so she acquired a master's degree in library science from the University of Denver. She has been a children's librarian since 1978 and is now Youth Services Manager for the Deschutes Public Libraries in central Oregon. Her storytelling performances have taken her across the United States, as well as to Kenya, New Zealand, Crete, and Scotland. The only thing that Heather is more passionate about than storytelling is her daughter, Jamie, whom she adopted in Vietnam in 1998.